BY ELIZABETH DREW

Washington Journal: The Events of 1973–1974
American Journal: The Events of 1976
Senator

SENATOR

Elizabeth Drew

SIMON AND SCHUSTER | NEW YORK

Published by Simon and Schuster
A Division of Gulf & Western Corporation
Simon & Schuster Building
Rockefeller Center
1230 Avenue of the Americas
New York, New York 10020

Most of the material in this book appeared originally in The New Yorker, *in slightly different form.*
Manufactured in the United States of America

1 2 3 4 5 6 7 8 9 10

Library of Congress Cataloging in Publication Data

Drew, Elizabeth.
Senator.

"Most of the material . . . appeared originally in The New Yorker, *in slightly different form."*
1. United States. Congress. Senate. 2. Culver, John C., date. I. Title.
JK1161.D65 328.73'07'1 79-596
ISBN 0-671-24843-X

ACKNOWLEDGMENTS

Once again, I am indebted to William Shawn of *The New Yorker* for his guidance and support. I am also grateful to Christine Haynes for her dedicated and valuable assistance.

SENATOR

Politics is the only forum in which we can resolve our differences. As long as equally worthy people have incompatible goals, somebody has to mediate—unless you want things decided by the whim of a dictator or unless you want to shoot it out. The politicians are our mediators.

—JOHN GARDNER

1

EACH of the one hundred members of the United States Senate at some point establishes a reputation within the institution by which his colleagues judge him and by which his effectiveness is measured. Some become known as mediocrities, some as well-meaning but ineffective, some as phonies, some as mavericks (a category that is broken down into useful mavericks, such as Wayne Morse was, and ignorable ones), a few are dismissed as jokes, and a few are taken seriously. Many work to obtain federal money and projects for their states, attend their committee meetings, and cast their votes on the Senate floor but have little impact on the institution or on national policy. Some senators establish themselves as powers through seniority or because of presumed expertise on a certain subject—a presumption that is not always well founded—but in the early 1970's, the Senate began to change, to the point where its members no longer needed seniority in order to have an impact. In 1978, at the age of forty-five, John C. Culver, a Democratic senator from Iowa, still in his first term, which had started in 1975, had already established a reputation as one of the most effective members of the Senate.

In the summer of 1978, I spent some time with Culver, in the Senate and in Iowa, talking with him and watching him formulate strategies, push his legislation, decide how to cast his votes, deal with his constituents, respond to the things that came at him, and cope with the extraordinary pressures that a senator faces. Watching Culver as he worked through the crosscurrents, hazards, complications, and pressures of Senate life, one could get a picture of that life, of what one senator actually does, and also of the workings of the Senate.

Culver is not a saint and he is not an ideologue. He is an unusual combination: a man with firm principles and beliefs who is also a practical politician—one who gets in there and does the hard work of legislating, of putting together coalitions, of mediating among the conflicting interests in this country, of making the whole thing go. Anyone who tries to do this has to keep in mind a lot of roiling objectives and somehow work it all out. Those who can do this thoughtfully, carefully, and courageously are rare—and essential. Among the other senators, Culver soon developed a reputation for brains, tenacity, integrity, shrewdness at picking his issues and skill at pushing them, and an ability to work with his colleagues. He was usually among a handful who voted against proposals that played to the crowds but that he dismissed as "demagogic." And what he accomplished he did in part through the sheer force of his personality and style. Even his size had something to do with it. Culver is a huge man: he is six feet two and easily weighs two hundred and fifty pounds. His broad, stocky body—he was a football star (fullback) at Harvard—had developed a slight paunch. He has a large head on a thick neck, and big hands. His voice is husky, and when turned up to full volume, sounds as if it were coming from a bullhorn. He has blond hair that is thinning in front, blue eyes, a wide nose, a mobile, expressive face, and a pink complexion that quickly turns red when he is moved to laughter or anger—which he is, easily and often. Culver has a powerful temper, and he can also be a very funny man. The temper may unsettle or antagonize associates or officials who have been its target, but, like his humor, it is an ingredient of his effectiveness, and it is also part of a deeper aspect of his personality. Culver is one of the few politicians of recent times who have been unashamed to feel, and to show, passion on the issues. One of Culver's Senate colleagues told me, "John's temper and his passion go together; and the temper gives the other members pause before taking him on." Moreover, because he is a big man with a big voice who says things forcefully, what he says as his temperature rises becomes magnified. Said an aide to another senator, "He does have a low flash point, but by and large it helps. He communicates his concern so devastatingly that people don't want to argue with him; the excesses get excused because of his effectiveness."

Other senators talked to me about Culver's perspective on himself and on the institution, his discipline, and the fact that, as several put it, "he is his own man." One, a Southern Democrat, said—and he was not talking about Culver's physical attributes—"You just can't knock him over." Several made the point that he is not one of the posturers in the place, and not one of those who feel compelled, as so many do, to rush to the floor or to the television cameras with a statement on just about everything, and said that this restraint adds to his effectiveness. One senator observed, "It's more important to know when to shut up than when to speak." It is not simply Culver's bulk or his temper, or even his mind, that causes him to have a certain impact on people who deal with him; he also has "presence." It is an atmosphere he establishes which suggests that when doing business with him one had better be well prepared, know what one is talking about, and not waste his time; it is a quality that emits an unspoken "Don't mess."

Culver is a modern, sophisticated man with several old-fashioned characteristics, political and personal. On those occasions when he takes to the Senate floor for a major speech, it is an event: he lets go in a stem-winding style that one associates with the Senate of a hundred years ago. One member of the House—where Culver served five terms—has said that Culver is the one person he knows who gets more articulate the angrier he gets. He can be impatient and demanding, and sometimes verges on playing the bully with officials who come before his committees with testimony he considers ill-prepared or misleading. He can also be warm and sensitive. He can be talkative or contemplative, hyperactive or peaceful (but not, it seems, for very long). He can be raucous or reserved—almost shy—and when he is being kidded he can blush and even become tongue-tied (but, again, not for very long). He can be profane or choirboy polite. And there is an unaffectedness about him—a simple, and sometimes startling, directness.

2

MONDAY, JULY 10, 1978: Congress is returning today from a ten-day Fourth of July recess. Culver was in Iowa over the Fourth and then, with his wife, Ann, and a few other senators and their wives, he went to Alaska to study the question of how much of the land there should be placed under federal protection. The trip was gruelling, and Culver has flown all night to get back to Washington, so he is very tired. Now, at ten o'clock, sitting in his office, Room 344 of the Russell Senate Office Building, he scans a summary prepared by his staff of press clippings from Iowa which have accumulated in his absence. Some refer both to him and to his Senate colleague from Iowa, Dick Clark. Culver reads aloud an item summarizing a letter to the editor: "Would J.C.C. and Clark defect to Russia rather than make anti-Communism speech?" He rolls his eyes upward and says wearily, "Welcome home."

Culver was first elected to the House in 1964, in the Democratic landslide of that year. Two years later, he was one of two out of six Democrats from Iowa who were reëlected to the House, and thereafter he built his congressional district into an increasingly safe one. Before he ran for the House, Culver served for a year as a legislative assistant to Senator Edward M. Kennedy, who had been a close friend since they were freshmen at Harvard. Upon graduating from Harvard, Culver spent a year as a Lionel de Jersey Harvard Scholar at Cambridge University, living in John Harvard's rooms there; then he served thirty-nine months in the Marines, and after that he went to Harvard Law School. During his last year at law school, he helped Kennedy in his race for the Senate in 1962. His plan had been that when he finished law school that year, he would return to Iowa, to practice law and go into politics (his father had been active in Republican politics), but Kennedy persuaded him to come to Washington for a while.

Culver took a lot of kidding about 1972, when, having served in the House of Representatives for eight years, he declined, after surveying the political situation, to run for the Senate against the Republican incumbent, Jack Miller; Clark, who had served as Culver's administrative assistant for seven years and had been preparing to run for Culver's House seat if Culver did run for the Senate, made the Senate race instead, and won. (Culver first met Clark in 1963, when Culver was preparing for his first race for the House. Clark, who was teaching Russian history at Upper Iowa University, in Fayette, was deeply involved in the techniques of local political organization, and Culver enlisted him.) Some of Culver's political associates say that his assessment of the 1972 situation was correct: that, because Clark did not have an established political record for Miller to campaign against, and was unknown and not expected to win, Miller did not campaign as hard against him as he would have against Culver. In 1973, when Harold Hughes, a Democrat, who was then Iowa's other senator, announced that he would not run for reëlection in 1974, some of Culver's friends, including Kennedy, sent Culver a telegram asking for the name of his current administrative assistant, so that they could make a contribution to his Senate campaign. Culver made the race and won.

Now, in his office, Culver reads a summary of another story, about his having voted, shortly before the recess, against severing all diplomatic and economic relations with Cuba. Also, Culver was one of four senators who voted against an amendment offered by Jesse Helms, a very conservative Republican from North Carolina, to prohibit any foreign aid or the sale or transfer of any goods to Cambodia, Vietnam, Uganda, or Cuba. And he was one of twenty-two senators who voted against a five-percent cut in foreign assistance. Of late, in a reaction to the adoption by the voters of California of Proposition 13, cutting property taxes drastically, Congress has adopted a number of such amendments to make across-the-board cuts. On the day after the foreign-aid votes, Culver voted against an across-the-board cut in an appropriations bill for the Treasury Department, and also against an amendment to delete funds that the Department planned to use to keep track of the traffic in firearms. Both of these proposals carried. All of Culver's colleagues from Iowa in the House voted to delete funds to monitor firearms, and so did Clark in the Senate. In 1967, during the domestic turmoil over the Vietnam War, Culver was one of sixteen members of the House to vote against a bill that made desecration of the American flag a federal offense.

When I was talking to Culver before the recess, I asked him why he had decided to vote against the Helms amendment on aid to Vietnam, Cuba, and the rest. He replied, "It hadn't been reviewed. It was modified on the floor, so no one knew the full ramifications of it. Besides, it's another example of denying the President flexibility in international matters, and things are in such flux that there are some situations where Presidential discretion is valid. Our policies towards certain countries can change within a week or ten days. It shows the importance of having a chance to exploit opportunities. I think when you're faced with an arrogant disregard of the law on the part of an Administration, that's one thing, but this was just demagoguing about a list." Then he talked about his vote against making the five-per-cent cut in assistance. "We're giving about one-fourth of one per cent of our gross national product to foreign aid," he said. "It's one of the worst records on foreign aid of all the industrial nations. I think, too, that the third-world problem in the year 2000 will be every bit as great a threat to our security as the U.S.-Soviet balance. I think that the threat that's represented in terms of our ability to deal with third-world problems—food, development, trade, the potential instability—is going to make it impossible to maintain ourselves as an isolated island of affluence, and I think that that transcends some of our more immediate preoccupations."

Now Culver reads a summary of an editorial in the Des Moines *Register:* "Doesn't agree with recommendations to retaliate against Soviet newsmen for charges brought against U.S. newsmen." Culver has reason to be grateful for the *Register*, a liberal paper that reaches the entire state of Iowa. I remark on the many statements being made by politicians about the current trials of dissidents in the Soviet Union. He tells me that he thinks that the United States government should respond—expressing its adherence to certain values—but that it should do so with sophistication and discipline; and that he worries that at a certain point the statements by the politicians may not be helpful to the dissidents' cause. He says, "God, can you imagine anyone in

Congress standing up and saying anything but 'Hang the Wilmington Ten' if the Soviets did anything like that?" Next, Culver reads a clipping of an editorial in the Storm Lake, Iowa, *Register* that says he and Clark "are following the desire of the big unions." He says to me, "Isn't it wonderful to get back?"

The Senate has gone into session at eleven this morning to begin debate on the military-procurement bill, an annual bill to authorize funds for research and development and purchase of major weapons and to set the manpower levels for the armed forces. Culver, who is a member of the Senate Armed Services Committee, plans to offer an amendment stipulating that the Navy should in the future build no big aircraft carriers beyond the one—the twelfth in the fleet—that is provided for in the bill. His argument is that the giant carriers are too vulnerable, and that the Navy should be pushed into reliance on smaller, more flexible ship-and-plane combinations. The Administration opposed the new carrier, a nuclear one, which has strong support in both the Senate and the House; but the Senate Armed Services Committee has authorized it, and the Administration has not tried to get it removed from this bill. (The Administration's plans did call for one more large carrier, but a conventionally powered one.) Culver has decided that there is no likelihood that a majority of the Senate would vote to delete funds for the new carrier, and has chosen the next-strongest proposal.

This is typical of Culver's legislative style. He does not take on a large number of issues, and those that he takes on tend to be ones that make an important point—and also ones on which he feels he has a reasonable chance of winning. One of his associates said to me, "He doesn't spread-eagle a lot. He gets enormously annoyed if he takes on something that doesn't result in something. He's not like some of the others. Take Hubert Humphrey, for example. If twenty-five of the fifty bills he introduced were never heard of again, he didn't give it another thought. Culver is anxious to know what the traction is before he starts." An aide to another senator said, "Culver has something of a genius for spotting an issue—for seeing something others may not have thought of—and for knowing which arguments will work best in debate, and then he makes his case better than the others, because he has worked harder and is better prepared." Culver's earliest big issues in the Senate were unconventional and against the grain. His maiden speech there, in 1975, was one in which he opposed a bill that would have restored the retired military status as an Air Force colonel of Alexander Butterfield, a former aide in the Nixon White House who was later named administrator of the Federal Aviation Administration. In 1975, Butterfield left the F.A.A. and sought reinstatement of his military status, which he had surrendered to take the civilian post, and the Senate Armed Services Committee approved a bill granting his request. Culver turned this into the issue of the preservation of civilian control over the government and made a speech that lasted a little over an hour. He pointed out that the statute establishing the F.A.A., which has jurisdiction over both civil and military airspace, specifically stated that the administrator should be a civilian. "We are talking about a constitutional principle as old as the Republic," he said. In this debate, he took on his own committee, including its chairman, John Stennis, Democrat of Mississippi, and he won. The bill was defeated.

The same year, Culver took on another issue that seemed obscure to most people at the time but that had significant consequences. He opposed the construction of a military base on Diego Garcia, a horseshoe-shaped atoll in the Indian Ocean. Culver offered an amendment stipulating that no money could be spent on the construction until 1976, and that by that time efforts would be made to negotiate with the Soviet Union about trying to prevent a military buildup in the area. He debated the issue at length on the Senate floor in July of 1975, and lost. He did not give up, however. Later in the year, he learned that the Ford Administration had misled the Senate by saying that the island was uninhabited—that in fact, pursuant to a secret arrangement with the British, from whom the United States had leased the island, all the inhabitants had been removed. In November, he won Senate approval of his amendment. In April, 1976, the Ford Administration reported that it had not yet approached the Soviet Union on the question, and it requested no further funds. The new Democratic Administration, in 1977, opened talks on demilitarization of the Indian Ocean. An aide to another senator says, "At first, everyone was wondering why Culver was bothering with a coral reef. Later, we understood." Culver's own staff was divided in its enthusiasm over this project, but Culver followed his instincts. Says one of Culver's staff members, "When others were saying 'Why are you bothering? Who's Diego Garcia—a dead Cuban revolutionary?' he was in there working at it."

Another early fight that Culver made over a seemingly obscure point—over whether Congress should buy a certain building on Capitol Hill, 400 North Capitol Street, for additional office space—occurred in 1976. Culver turned that into the issue of what he termed "the chaos and confusion" over the use of space on Capitol Hill. The Capitol is an archaically run place, and Culver had worked on this problem when he was a member of the House; after he reached the Senate, he proposed that a commission of outside experts be created to study such questions as how senators use their time, the utilization of space, and how to change the irrational bureaucratic system that theoretically manages the operation of Capitol Hill. The commission issued its report at the end of 1976. When Culver talked to me about it recently, he said that the commission "was primarily addressed to obsolete overlap." He continued, "We've got these various things being run by the Sergeant at Arms, the Secretary of the Senate, the Architect of the Capitol, the Majority Leader's Office. There are no space inventories. There's no rational central management of personnel. The Sergeant at Arms handles the flooring, the carpeting, and the furnishing of the Capitol, and the Architect handles the painting of the walls and ceiling." He pointed to a clock on a wall of his office and said, "If that clock doesn't work, one person fixes one part of it and one fixes another. People up here are sick of reform, but I think we're making some quiet progress on this. It isn't the sexiest topic, but we're trying to do some things that will make sense out of this place." In his fight against the purchase of the building, Culver took on one of the other great orators in the Senate—Ernest Hollings, Democrat of South Carolina. The resulting show was memorable. A Senate aide recalls, "It was like two deer with thirty-five-point antlers—kings of the herd—clashing. Culver won, and people still talk about the day Culver took on Hollings."

Culver's interest in the process by which Congress conducts its business as well as in the substantive results—and his understanding of the connection between the two—was also reflected in a provision that he got incorporated in some House reforms when he was serving in that body: it urged House committees to exercise "foresight" as well as "oversight." The provision said that the committees should keep abreast not only of current developments but of forecasts of future developments in their fields of jurisdiction, and consider when new legislation might be needed. The committees haven't much followed this guidance, but Culver was on to something. "One of the real problems we have with the legislative process," he said to me recently, "is that we're dealing with after-the-fact data that may be obsolete, and once we get the money for a program out the problem may have disappeared, and then we don't have any oversight. We just don't get out ahead of the curve. There are classic examples, like the failure to anticipate the baby boom and its implications in terms of schools, hospitals, jobs, the elderly—and then when the baby boom ends we're still building hospitals." In the early nineteen-seventies, Culver's interest in "futurology" led him to push for a state project called Iowa 2000—a program in which the citizens could participate in decisions about the future of the state. He worked with the governor, the state legislature, and the University of Iowa; there were local, regional, and state conferences, and the university is publishing the results. He has got the Senate to approve federal funds to encourage other states to undertake this sort of exercise. "The idea was to get maximum participation, not to have a blueprint imposed by a bunch of wise men," Culver says.

Culver's reputation for tenacity, established by his early fights, was enhanced by his fight, from 1976 on, to kill the B-1 bomber. "Maybe it's the fullback in him," an aide to another senator says. "When he spots something, he just piles right up the Senate." The fight over the B-1 was the biggest that Culver had taken on. Characteristically, he ascertained that he would have traction: that he had good, sustainable sources of information inside and outside the government; that there were divisions among defense professionals, including those within the Department of Defense, on the issue;

that he would have strong allies in the Senate; that he would have help from such places as Harvard and M.I.T., where he has good contacts.

Culver, in fact, gets around, and has a wide network of contacts: through past and present Harvard connections (he is a member of its Board of Overseers and of the senior advisory committee of the John F. Kennedy Institute of Politics there); through old friends in the House, with whom he has made it a point to keep in touch more than most senators do who have moved on from the House; through his connections with the Kennedy circle; and through his own wide range of friends—which includes Averell Harriman and old political pals from Iowa—around Washington. When Culver was in the House, he was seen as one of its more promising members—he served on the Foreign Affairs Committee and on a committee to reform House procedures, and he also headed the liberal Democratic Study Group—and was invited to join such organizations as the Trilateral Commission and to attend innumerable conferences. Moreover, members of Congress and their staffs, particularly if they are in a position to be effective and are astute enough to know how to do so, can become recipients of information from within the bureaucracy. Culver fought a series of battles on the B-1. First, he succeeded in putting through an amendment on the Senate floor—overturning the Armed Services Committee in the process—which delayed the spending of money to procure B-1s until February, 1977 (that is, until a new Administration might take office and have an opportunity to review the matter), and until the President certified that such expenditures were necessary. This procedural approach to a substantive issue—making something seem a matter of process, and therefore more reasonable than a frontal attack—is, again, characteristic of Culver's legislative style. It is extremely rare that a major weapons system is killed outright in Congress. Culver's amendment was not adopted in the Senate-House conference on the bill, but a version of it was later adopted as part of another bill. When President Carter, who had spoken on both sides of the B-1 issue during the Presidential primaries, was making up his mind on whether to go ahead with the bomber, Culver, on behalf of and at the behest of its congressional opponents, made the case to Carter against it. Carter eventually cancelled the plane.

In 1977, Culver fought the Carter Administration's plan to sell the highly sophisticated Airborne Warning and Control System (AWACS) to Iran, but the Administration secured enough support to win approval of the sale after various concessions had been made to Culver and his allies.

Culver is, of course, a junior member of the Armed Services Committee, and he is also one of a small minority of its members willing to challenge the Pentagon on major programs. He makes most of his fights on armed-services bills within the committee, and strictly limits the number of issues that he will take to the Senate floor afterward. "I always have something of a problem," he told me in a conversation before the recess. "I have to decide which issues to hit hard on and how to pick my shots, how to remain credible, not be irrelevant. You can't posture and fight in a knee-jerk way, and identify with every issue that comes along. It's hard enough to make these fights and still stay viable. The fights are very emotional; strong interests are involved. I try to approach it in a constructively critical way—to fight for a cost-effective defense. So I challenge where I don't think the military is doing enough to provide us with the proper readiness, and I challenge on excessive expenditures, like the B-1." Culver, who is proud of his service in the Marines, is not a conventional "dove." He talks frequently about a "cost-effective defense," and he does support certain increases in the Pentagon budget—especially measures to improve combat readiness through better maintenance and greater reliability of weapons.

"You can't go on the floor and just tear up what the committee has done," he says. "There are trade-offs. There are areas where you try to establish expertise and competence and where you think it's worth the expenditure of political capital, and you try to win on those. And once you've established some sense of your competence in that way, there are other areas where you can take something on and win. It's just like a lawyer in a town who establishes a reputation in the practice of law as someone who goes in and wins cases; then there are a lot of things he can establish without having to go into court. I think that's true in Congress, and in the executive. If they think that you're effective, think that you know what you're talking about, then you can be effective. But you have to be discriminating. You can't be posturing and predictable."

He talks frequently, and disparagingly, about policymakers and politicians who have never served in the armed forces and who seem eager for international confrontations and large-scale increases in expenditures for arms. He says, "It seems to me that the propensity for hawkishness is in direct proportion to how remote a person is from any military experience."

Culver is one of a group of senators who have been preparing to fight for Senate approval of a new Strategic Arms Limitation Talks (SALT) agreement—he is careful to say, "Provided it is a good agreement and one that is verifiable"—and the expectation is that he will play a major role. Meanwhile, there are other military issues, some of them related to SALT, some not, that he is pursuing. Among the amendments to the military-procurement bill which Culver succeeded in getting adopted within the Armed Services Committee this year was one that would delete a provision in existing law requiring that every large surface vessel proposed to Congress be nuclear-powered, or the President must explain why it is not. This provision is known as "the Rickover provision," after its chief sponsor, Admiral Hyman Rickover. In 1976, Rickover, himself an intimidating man, and Culver tangled over the subject in an Armed Services Committee hearing—Rickover made the mistake of challenging Culver's credentials for dealing with it—and Culver thereupon sponsored an amendment to repeal the Rickover provision, which carried in the committee and also on the Senate floor. "That got his attention," Culver says to me today. The amendment was dropped in the bargaining over the bill between conferees representing the Senate and the House, but this year Culver got it into the bill again.

A proposal Culver offered in the committee this year which was not adopted was an amendment to provide for a study, to be submitted by the President, of the impact of nuclear exchanges of various levels of magnitude. This was opposed by Henry Jackson, Democrat of Washington and second-ranking member of the committee, who has been essentially a defender of military budget requests and a critic of SALT. In the committee meeting in which Jackson opposed the study of nuclear effects, Culver demanded, "What are you afraid of? What are you afraid of?" But he was voted down. "Isn't that interesting?" Culver says to me today. "The idea was to make the attractions of nuclear war a little less persuasive. Isn't that unbelievable?" Now Culver is planning to try to persuade Stennis to permit the General Legislation Subcommittee, which Culver heads, and which has jurisdiction over the subject of civil defense, to hold hearings on nuclear effects. Recently, there have been reports that the Administration would ask for an additional two billion dollars over five years for a civil-defense program, and Culver has made the connection in his mind between the possible new emphasis on civil defense and the whole argument over the strategic-arms balance. Culver says, "We need to increase the public understanding in both the United States and the Soviet Union of the dangers of nuclear war, by drawing upon a wide and diverse group of technically qualified sources, both outside and within the government, who can address themselves to this question. This will make it clear that the concept of a 'limited' nuclear war is absurd."

Referring to reports and warnings issued by the more vigorous critics of SALT, Culver says, "One of their major pegs is that the Soviets do not share our strategic-nuclear-doctrine concepts of deterrence and mutual assured destruction. These critics cite Soviet military literature that talks about fighting and surviving, or even winning, a nuclear war. But we have the same problem on our side. We have people in our own military who talk in the same vein about a nuclear war. We have always taken the rather snobbish attitude that we would educate those 'barbarians' about sophisticated concepts of strategic warfare. But one of the problems of the U.S.-Soviet relationship is that the Soviets' tactics, doctrine, strategy, force structure are so much a part of the special geography and history of their country. They've been landlocked, and we've been a sea power; they've been invaded several times, and we've never known comparable death and destruction. They have potentially hostile powers on their borders, and we don't. One of the objectives of the SALT talks should be to bring about a greater degree of understanding of these things by the two nations. The point of holding hearings on nuclear effects is that I think the more you can dramatize the horrors of nuclear war the more you can demonstrate the insanity of contemplating a 'successful' one. I believe that we should be making determined efforts to achieve greater agreement on strategic doctrine, and a greater shared awareness of nuclear effects will help bring that about. And then we can have a more realistic view of civil defense—of whether a one- or two-billion-dollar expenditure makes any sense in that context."

Culver tells me that he has been urging Stansfield Turner, the director of the Central Intelligence Agency, to declassify and make public a report by the intelligence community on the Soviets' civil defense. "The various reports on what they are actually doing have been somewhat mixed," he says. "Our official position has been that what we have heard they are doing and what we could conceive of their doing could be offset by a retargeting of our missiles—that there's no way you can rationally protect yourself from unacceptable damage. They've got their pamphlets, and we have ours. They've got their signs in their subways, and we have ours. The official line here has been that we'll keep an eye on it and if it looks serious we'll retarget. But the far right says the Soviets' civil defense is getting so substantial that they might feel they could safely launch a nuclear war. I've tried in the committee to keep us from throwing money at the problem. When you get into this military stuff, you talk about capabilities and perceptions and intentions. You should deal with capabilities, and not intentions. You have to be able to deal with capabilities even if the intentions are benign. Perceptions are important, of course; they can cast a long shadow. In our internal debates, we often create our own perception of weakness—we create a self-fulfilling prophecy that comes around and bites us in the tail."

Now Culver ascertains through a telephone

conversation with Charles Stevenson, his chief legislative assistant for the Armed Services Committee work—he has two aides to deal with such work—that his aircraft-carrier amendment will not come up until tomorrow. He is relieved: he is tired, and needs more time to get prepared. Also, he wants to have some time for Stevenson to talk the amendment over with members of the committee staff, so that Culver will have some indication of how Stennis will react when he presents the idea to him. Culver has been giving consideration to offering the amendment for some time, but he has not yet informed the committee about it, so as to avoid giving opponents there or in the Pentagon much time to work against it.

Shortly after noon, Culver reviews with various staff members the status of other issues he is working on. According to Senate rules, senators are to serve on two major committees and one minor one, but Culver, during the Ninety-fifth Congress (1977–78) is on three major committees—Armed Services, Judiciary, and Environment and Public Works—as well as a minor one, Small Business, and he heads four subcommittees. This is a result of one of the fights he got into with Senate Majority Leader Robert Byrd, Democrat of West Virginia, at the beginning of this Congress, in 1977. Culver, along with Kennedy, Senator Edmund S. Muskie, Democrat of Maine, and a number of other Democrats, backed Hubert Humphrey over Byrd for Majority Leader. They knew that Humphrey did not have much of a chance—that he was ill and that Byrd had been working hard for the job for years—but they felt that Humphrey represented more closely what they stood for as Democrats than the more conservative Byrd did. (Moreover, there had been a long-standing rivalry between Byrd and Kennedy, who had been the Democratic Whip for two years, until Byrd defeated him.) After Humphrey lost, there was a fight over the question of whether Humphrey or Byrd would be chairman of the Senate Democratic caucus. The chairmanship of the House caucus is held by someone other than the Majority Leader, and the group felt that this should be the rule in the Senate, too; besides, Culver and his allies were seeking a way to make Humphrey a member of the leadership group that meets with the President at the White House, and thus a conduit for the liberals. Byrd won the caucus chairmanship, but an arrangement was made whereby Humphrey joined the delegation to the White House. Then there was a fight over the question of whether Byrd himself or the entire caucus would name the members of the Steering Committee, which makes committee assignments, and the Policy Committee, which schedules legislation. Byrd once more prevailed, but a procedure proposed by Culver to make the selection system more democratic was adopted for future years. The next fight was over the question of whether there would be an individual vote by the caucus on each committee chairman. On that, Culver and his allies won.

In the course of all this, Culver exploded in the caucus, breaking down the fraternal façade by which senators set so much store, and saying out loud—very loud—things that a number of them had been quietly saying to each other. He shouted, "Any time anyone around here suggests any reform, it is taken as a personal affront." He railed against new senators who, he said, had campaigned saying, "Elect me; I'll go down there and change some things," and, now that they were fresh off the hustings, were suddenly quiet, more concerned about their committee assignments than about reform. "Here's your moment!" he roared at them. Then, when James Allen, the very conservative senator from Alabama, was proposed for a vacancy on the Judiciary Committee—an appointment that would have tipped the balance of the committee to the conservative side—another fight ensued. Culver accused Byrd to his face of trying to "buy Allen off." (Allen was one of the senators most expert at causing delay in floor legislation.) As a consequence, eventually both Culver and Allen were named to the committee.

Culver puffs on a cigar as his aides review what will be coming up shortly on the floor and in his committees, and the situation on a bill involving endangered species which Culver will manage on the Senate floor, and which is expected to be scheduled for debate within the next week. The endangered-species issue is an emotional one, and this will be the first major bill that Culver has managed. The Endangered Species Act of 1973 required that the government draw up a list of fish, wildlife, and plants considered to be in danger of extinction, and prohibited federal projects that might jeopardize them. The result was a series of confrontations between environmentalists and builders. The most spectacular example was the Tellico Dam, which was being built by the Tennessee Valley Authority and was ordered halted by the Supreme Court in June, after it was discovered that the project would impinge on the critical habitat of a three-inch fish called the snail darter. At that point, the dam was nearly completed. Culver was already deeply involved in the endangered-species issue because the law is scheduled to expire at the end of this September and he heads the Resource Protection Subcommittee of the Environment and Public Works Committee, which has jurisdiction over it. Encouraged by his staff, and persuaded that the number of such disputes under the act was going to grow, thus making the act vulnerable, he began to work out a mechanism by which the conflicts might be resolved. Culver has been a strong environmentalist, but he also figured that unless the act was made more flexible it would be in trouble when it came up for reauthorization—that it might be eviscerated or even killed. "We were trying to get out ahead of the problem," Culver told me. "There isn't a lot of political reward for that. So we spend most of our time here dealing with the political pressures in terms of short-range panaceas." He continued, "The act has polarized the environmentalists and the builders, and that affects the money that comes into your campaign chests." Culver felt that as chairman of the subcommittee he had to try to find a solution that would insure the survival of the Endangered Species Act. He carefully, methodically built a consensus: he worked with Howard Baker, of Tennessee, the Senate Minority Leader, and the second-ranking Republican member of the Environment and Public Works Committee, on a solution, and eventually persuaded both the subcommittee and the full committee to support it. The bill has been reported by the committee unanimously. Culver's solution is to establish a seven-member interagency committee to resolve disputes that arise under the act. The committee could provide exemptions that would allow a project to go ahead, but its procedures would be heavily weighted in favor of the species. Culver has told me that some of the environmental groups assured him and his staff that they recognized the political realities the act had encountered, and that the compromise was a "constructive" approach, which they would support. "The problem is," Culver says, "that some of those assurances didn't stay stuck, and the newsletters and the press releases went out saying this was a know-nothing attack on the ecosystem."

Now Culver's aides tell him that this week the Juvenile Delinquency Subcommittee, which he chairs, of the Judiciary Committee will draw up—"mark up"—a bill tightening the regulation of PCP (phencyclidine, or "angel dust"); that the full Judiciary Committee will meet to vote on certain bills; that a water-pollution-and-soil-conservation program Culver is sponsoring will be coming up soon, as will a highway bill, for which Culver is seeking a provision that will allow some of the funds set aside for the construction of bridges to be used for bridges on rural roads as well as for those on federal highways. Culver is planning to go to Iowa this weekend, and one staff member tells Culver that when he does he will be able to announce a fifteen-thousand-dollar grant to Des Moines for the study of noise pollution. There is some discussion about what stops he should make during the trip to Iowa.

Tomorrow morning, Culver will have to chair a hearing of the Resource Protection Subcommittee on whether the National Environmental Policy Act, which requires federal agencies that undertake certain kinds of projects to prepare a statement of the environmental impact of their activities, should apply to international transactions. Senator Adlai Stevenson, Democrat of Illinois and chairman of the International Finance Subcommittee of the Banking, Housing, and Urban Affairs Committee, has proposed that the activities of the Export-Import Bank, which lends money to companies to help them sell their products overseas, be exempted from the act. American businesses are concerned that if they have to wait for the filing of such reports they will be put at a competitive disadvantage against foreign companies. Stevenson's proposal has been approved by the full Banking Committee. The White House has asked Culver, whose subcommittee has jurisdiction over the Environmental Policy Act, to delay action on Stevenson's proposal until the Administration can come up with a position on the question, and Culver has obliged by scheduling a hearing. But the Administration has been in disarray on the issue, because the numerous interested federal agencies have been unable to come up with a united position. Culver has his own concern with this issue. "The Export-Import Bank just made a loan to the government of the Philippines to build a nuclear plant right on an earthquake fault," he has told me. Now Kathi Korpon, a staff member who works on matters before the Environment and Public Works Committee, tells him that tomorrow the Administration, which has already been granted a postponement of the hearing and said it would have its position worked out by tomorrow, will testify against the Stevenson amendment, but doesn't have its own position worked out yet.

"So what are they coming up here for?" Culver asks somewhat testily. "To tell us they don't know?"

Mrs. Korpon explains that the Administration now has a position almost ready, but the President hasn't cleared it, and he is leaving later this week for Europe, for an economic summit conference in Bonn.

Culver asks, "What kind of catalogue of horror stories do we have for me to use in the hearing?"

Mrs. Korpon mentions the nuclear power plant in the Philippines.

"Are there any others?" Culver asks. "I've been using that one. Can you get me some more by tomorrow?"

Another staff member tells Culver about a bill Culver has pending before the Small Business Committee, relaying information he has gathered on interagency bickering over what the Administration's position should be on the bill, and Culver suggests that he make a call to a member of the White House congressional-liaison staff. "Tell him it's something I care a lot about," he says. They talk about the status of a bill that Culver has introduced to provide for the payment of attorneys' fees for small businesses when they are involved in litigation over government regulations, and about another Culver bill, this one to revise the United States Olympic Committee charter. (Culver served on the President's Commission on Olympic Sports, which issued a report in 1977.) Then Culver discusses with his staff whether or not to go ahead with sending a letter to Russell Long, Democrat of Louisiana and chairman of the Senate Finance Committee, to urge consideration of a Senate resolution he has introduced expressing disapproval of the President's recent action raising the amount of beef that may be imported into the United States. On this, as on some of the other issues, Culver asks staff members what they think the vote in the committee will be—how certain senators might line up. Culver says that he is reluctant to go ahead with the beef-import issue if it will amount to no more than a gesture. He asks a staff member how many co-sponsors he now has, and is told he has twenty-one. The conclusion is that, between those senators who are concerned about beef imports and those who want to cast a vote against Carter, the resolution might carry on the Senate floor. A staff member points out that Culver is scheduled to meet with some cattlemen in Iowa this weekend, and it would be good to be able to talk about the letter to Long. Culver decides to go ahead with it. The meeting proceeds, and one can see Culver wearying as the staff throws ever more details and issues at him, yet he keeps raising a number of questions himself.

Now George Jacobson, who also works for Culver on matters before the Environment and Public Works Committee, tells him that over the weekend Senator Gaylord Nelson, Democrat of Wisconsin, has come out against his endangered-species compromise and might offer an amendment to kill it. Nelson and Culver are close friends, and Culver is surprised. He again rolls his eyes upward. "My buddy," he says. "Thanks for the call, Gaylord." Nelson has been a strong environmentalist since long before such a stand was fashionable, and now Culver and his staff must worry about whether Nelson's move will cause environmental groups to oppose Culver's compromise. Culver breaks off this conversation to phone Charles Stevenson, who is on the Senate floor, to ask how the military-procurement bill is progressing and what has happened on his proposed aircraft-carrier amendment, and then he returns to the conversation about the endangered-species bill. He is concerned about getting caught in what he calls the cross fire between Nelson and John Stennis, who will sponsor an amendment to weaken the Endangered Species Act. A few other matters are discussed, and the meeting with the staff members ends.

After the staff members leave, Culver reaches for another cigar—he keeps a box of them on a table by his desk—and says to me, "Isn't that a lot? It's too much, isn't it? And that's just what lands in your field, it's not a matter of chasing and going. God, it's too much." Culver picks his big issues carefully, but the simple fact that he has a state to represent and committees to serve on and subcommittees to chair—and that he takes these jobs seriously—provides him with a very large agenda. He orders lunch at his desk, and goes over a four-page memorandum prepared by one of his staff members on the question of extending the time for ratification of the Equal Rights Amendment. Yesterday, there was a demonstration in Washington in favor of extending the seven-year deadline, which is due to expire next March, and this afternoon he is to meet with a pro-extension delegation from Iowa, which ratified the amendment in 1972.

Culver's office is rather ordinarily furnished with large brown leather chairs and sofa and a green carpet. There are photographs of his family around—the Culvers have four children—and on his desk is a very large ear of corn encased in Lucite. "Harold Hughes gave that to me," Culver remarks. "We explain that it must have been a drought year." Over the mantel is a painting of a Victorian building that Culver himself restored in McGregor, Iowa—a small town on the Mississippi River, in the northeast corner of the state. Culver maintains a home there, in addition to one in Washington. On the mantel are a drawing of a showboat on the Mississippi River; a framed poem, "Song of the Great River," which was written in 1973 by Paul Engle, the former head of the University of Iowa's International Writing Program, for the tricentennial celebration, arranged by Culver and held in McGregor, of the discovery of the upper Mississippi by Marquette and Joliet. There is also a framed saying:

> Until you've been in politics
> you've never really been alive
> it's rough and sometimes it's
> dirty and it's always hard
> work and tedious details
> But, it's the only sport
> for grownups—all other
> games are for kids.
>
> —HEINLEIN.

And there are on the mantel busts of John F. Kennedy and Robert F. Kennedy, and a collection of miniature pigs that Culver has gathered in the course of his travels around the world. On the walls are rice-paper drawings he bought during a trip to China last year.

Outside Culver's own office is the usual warren that makes up a Senate office suite. There are five rooms, three of them subdivided by plywood partitions. About twenty people, including staff members and summer internes, work in these rooms;

seven others handle mail in a building a half block away; and eleven work for Culver on committee matters in other offices in the two Senate office buildings. The office suite houses a chief assistant, Dick Oshlo, whose job it is to run the place; five legislative assistants, who follow various issues (and one of whom, Mike Naylor, is in general charge); Culver's press secretary, Don Brownlee; receptionists; his personal secretary, Pat Sarcone; other secretaries; and general office assistants. Culver also has two senior staff members: Park Rinard, who was once Grant Wood's personal secretary and then was Harold Hughes' closest adviser; and Fred Holborn, who was Culver's tutor at Harvard, and who worked for John Kennedy in the Senate and in the White House. (There are two Grant Wood drawings in Culver's outer offices.) In addition, Culver maintains four offices in Iowa, where a total of ten people work. The Iowa offices handle most of the casework for constituents—difficulties with Social Security or veterans' benefit checks, inquiries about Veterans Administration hospitals, applications for appointments to military academies, and problems with federal programs—and matters they cannot resolve are sent on to Washington. One Senate aide estimates that approximately one-fourth of every senator's job consists of taking care of state interests and casework.

Culver's five legislative assistants try their best to keep up with the legislation that is of direct interest to their senator, and also with everything else that is happening on the Senate floor. They try to know what is in each bill and amendment that might come up, but they can't always do so; besides, a number of amendments come up without any warning. The legislative assistants can follow the debate either by going to the Senate or by listening to a squawk box that broadcasts to the offices what is happening on the floor. Senators tend not to stay around the chamber except during debate on bills in which they have a direct interest, so they are as likely as not to arrive for a roll call without knowing what the precise issue is. They find out, and get recommendations on how to vote, from their legislative assistants, from other senators whose views they respect, and on occasion from an assistant to another senator. Most often, they know instinctively what to do once they hear what the issue is or who is sponsoring the amendment. Culver has told me that only about twenty per cent of the roll calls are close questions. The scale of the Senate staff, which has grown dramatically in the last decade or so, is, in a circular way, both a symptom and a cause of the increasing complexity of a senator's job. The staff has grown as a result of the increasing number of issues in which Congress has become involved, and the growth of the staff has, in turn, increased the number of issues in which Congress becomes involved. Senators tend to hire bright, aggressive young people who get satisfaction from suggesting ideas and seeing them carried out. This puts pressure on the senators to introduce bills or offer amendments or raise questions in order to satisfy a staff member some percentage of the time. The growth in staff has helped senators develop expertise in what they deal with, and to be more of a match for the executive branch, but it has also increased the senators' work load and has been a force for extending debate. Some senators are known for being influenced, or even run, by aggressive staff members; Culver seeks the advice of members of his staff, listens to them, but does not give them a great deal of running room.

As Culver and I sit in his office having lunch, he talks to me about his staff. "To have good, nice, capable staff—you can't have any better politics than that. A lot of people who come to work on the Hill believe that to be successful in politics you have to be Machiavellian and devious, where in fact those who will be most successful are more often those who are thoughtful, considerate, and straight." He continues, "It's so hard to demand high standards of performance and still not intimidate your staff or freeze their performance, because they're afraid of making mistakes—to achieve a combination of having them be careful and also creative." One of Culver's characteristics, noted by his friends, is objectivity about himself. As he talks now about the staff, this comes out. "I know I can be hyper and intimidating and aggressive, and I have to be careful not to expect too much of them. They can be bright and competent, but they don't all necessarily have the range of knowledge or the peripheral vision that you need up here. You have to be careful that they don't see themselves as failing when they fall short. You forget the importance of peer needs—how well they're liked by the rest of the staff, whether they have a date, and so on. I get to the point where I'm so driven and preoccupied and fulfilled in lots of ways—you know, 'Let's take the hill!'—that I forget about their needs. You get so driven that you're not likely to sense their need to have their own personal time. And we do demand and extract a lot in terms of hours."

Culver is a thorough man himself, and one day recently, when a staff member was handing me armloads of material to read up on, he remarked, "When you work for John Culver, you learn to be thorough." He is demanding of his staff and loses his temper with them, but he also kids around with them. About once a month, he has a breakfast for them, to which another senator comes and talks. Culver has something of a reputation for being difficult to work for, but this, and his reputation for having a temper—like many of the reputations that are set afloat in Washington—seems somewhat exaggerated and oversimplified. There is, in general, a fair amount of turnover on Capitol Hill, as staff members move on in their careers. It appears that Culver had more turnover in the House than he has had since he came to the Senate, and in any event he has a number of aides who have been with him for some time. It seems that if they get the hang of his temperament—and if they meet his exacting standards—they find his office one of the more interesting and enjoyable places to work. Culver's objectivity about himself also comes out when he discusses his temper—which he freely admits to having and can consider quite clinically. "I talk about it openly with the staff," he has told me. "I know when I've been unfair. I know when I take a minor point and bang it and bang it—belabor it and magnify it." Culver is detached enough to be able to say to a staff member later on that he knows he got more upset than he should have. His temper is not a simple or uncontrollable reaction. "My campaign opponents always think of it as a 'weakness' on my part that they can exploit—by goading me in debates, and the like—but it's never worked," he says. "There are things I feel strongly about. In the Marine Corps, in football—every place I've been, I felt strongly about it. You reach a critical mass and it comes out 'temper.' " He was once asked, in a TV interview in Iowa, whether reports that he had a temper were true. He said he supposed they were. What, he was asked, are the kinds of things that set it off? "Actually," he replied, "I handle it on a case-by-case basis."

At three-thirty, ten women from Iowa come into Culver's office to talk with him about the E.R.A. extension. There are three children with them. A member of Culver's staff has told me that they try to arrange for him to see as many as possible of the constituents who come to Washington, and that they try to schedule such meetings for the afternoons, because committee meetings are held in the morning and, ordinarily, the Senate does not meet until the afternoon—and it is easier to break away from the Senate floor than from a committee meeting. If Culver can't meet with the constituents, one of his assistants does; similarly, the assistants may stand in for him at the many trade-association receptions where some representation seems obligatory. Many politicians in Washington are virtually obsequious with constituents; several are polite but have a patronizing attitude toward them. Culver probably would not know how to be obsequious, nor does one get any sense that he feels patronizing. He is usually polite, but he has something of a reputation for being blunt on occasion—more blunt than most politicians are.

Culver himself, in the course of talking about the pressures of public opinion on politicians, recently told me of one such incident. It occurred in April of this year, on the day that the Senate was to vote on the second Panama Canal Treaty. Culver recalled, "I went out on the steps of the Senate to be photographed with a group from Iowa—it was a church group of teen-agers, with five or six chaperons. We were going to vote in about two hours on the second Panama Canal Treaty, and the Des Moines *Register's* Iowa Poll the weekend before had shown that only thirty per cent of the people in Iowa were in favor of the treaty. My staff had told me that the group wanted to talk to me about human rights and foreign aid and so forth. When I got out there, I said, 'Before you ask me any questions, I have a question for you.' I said, 'How many of you know what my position is on the Panama Canal?' There was sort of a pause, and then two or three hands went up—out of a group of eighteen or twenty people. I said, 'Are you sure you know what my position is?' And one of the chaperons said, 'We of course *hope* you're going to vote *for* it.' I said, 'Well, I came out in November, 1977, in Iowa in support of those treaties, and I got nothing but a drumbeat of steady criticism and ads and everything else against me for it. And, a month ago, I voted for the first treaty. If you people, who are supposedly the most dedicated group in support of those treaties, still have no idea of my position and don't make a conscientious effort to inform yourselves, and, moreover, smugly assume I'm going to vote for them or you'll be upset, how do you expect people like me to remain here very long voting that way? And how could you, as counsellors, bring this group out, supposedly on a political workshop, when we're taking one of the most historic votes ever taken here, and yet fail to inform them about this vote?' " For Culver, the incident dramatized, he told me, "why it's so difficult to get people to do the right thing." He said, "The interest group that is against something is disciplined, marshalled, mobilized, informed, and organized, with computerized mailings and propaganda and newsletters and visitations and all the rest, and is obsessed with that one issue. And, of course, that fact is not lost sight of by anybody up here, no matter what the issue is. It happens on gun control, abortion—you name it. And on the other side of the ledger is that amorphous constituency that wants you to do 'the right thing.' "

Culver is nearly exhausted by now, but he greets the E.R.A. delegation jovially. Once his visitors are seated in his office, he explains his fatigue by telling them a bit about his trip to Alaska, and says, "My head feels like a vegetable."

Minnette Doderer, a state senator, who just lost a primary campaign for lieutenant governor, explains that they are there to discuss extension of the time for ratification of the E.R.A. "You O.K.?" she asks.

"My natural inclinations are clear from the record," Culver replies (he voted for the Equal Rights

Amendment), and he continues, "But I want some more time to study it." He has got conflicting information from staff members on the issue of whether or not, if the time for ratification is extended, states should also be permitted to rescind their votes to approve, and he wants time to think it through. He suggests that the group leave some material with him. Mrs. Doderer tells him, "We do not want rescission." Culver asks her to send him the best arguments against permitting rescission, and to mark the letter "Personal," and tells her that he will take up the question with his staff.

Mrs. Doderer says, "We need you, we need you badly."

Mrs. Doderer's campaign loss is generally attributed to opposition by anti-abortionists, and now Culver turns to her and says, "Minnette, you and I have talked about single-issue politics. How do you distinguish this issue from other single-issue matters—gun control, abortion?" Culver recently gave a speech to the Wisconsin State Democratic Convention on single-issue politics, in which he said, "Strident and self-righteous groups of voters are proliferating in number and narrowing in focus." He said that in the past politicians could count on the support of groups not each of which would agree with them every time, and "being 'right' on most of the issues most of the time was more than enough." Now, he went on, "for each narrow, self-defined lobby . . . the worth of every public servant is measured by a single litmus test of ideological purity. Taken together, the tests are virtually impossible for any officeholder who hopes to keep both his conscience and his constituency."

Mrs. Doderer replies to his question by saying that the difference between the E.R.A. group and the others is that "we're not out to get anyone."

Culver responds, "Didn't I read in the paper this morning where people at yesterday's rally were saying 'Off with their heads'?" Culver is frowning now, and one gets the feeling that he is holding something in.

Then he turns to the children and asks, "Would you vote against me in the next election if I didn't vote the way you want me to on one issue even if I voted right on other issues?"

A boy who is twelve years old says, "No. It would depend on your entire record, and your opponent's record."

Culver smiles broadly. "Well, that's great," he says. "You'd see how I voted on foreign aid, energy, and so on? And you'd kind of make a balance of the issues? Well, good for you."

Mrs. Doderer says, "If you're wrong on one issue, you're usually wrong on a lot of issues, and if you're right on one issue, you're right on others."

Culver replies, "But 'right' and 'wrong' are, like beauty, in the eye of the beholder."

Another woman says, "Senator, I feel we were put on the defensive as a one-issue group. I don't think that's true. We'll be back to lobby you on other issues if you like."

Culver breaks the tension by smiling and saying, nicely, "Well, good for you. That's fine." Then he shows the group some of the items in his office—explaining where each of the miniature pigs came from—and poses with the visitors while Don Brownlee takes pictures. He autographs some photographs of himself for them and thanks them for coming by.

After the meeting, he says to me, "Wasn't that kid just great?"

Then he drops in on a birthday party for a staff member in one of the outer offices. A big subject at the party is that the Culver and Clark offices' combined softball team is supposed to play the Kennedy office team tomorrow evening. "Let's keep it low-key that I might play," Culver tells the staff, smiling. He pauses. "For one thing, I might not." Pause. "If Kennedy gets wind of the fact that I might come, he'll show up." Pause. "And then I'll have to show up."

At five-thirty, Culver is told by George Jacobson that Nelson definitely plans to oppose his endangered-species proposal. Jacobson says that he has been talking with staffs of other senators—Kennedy, and Gary Hart, Democrat of Colorado—to "test the waters" and see how much support Nelson might have. Dick Oshlo, who used to work for Culver on the Environment and Public Works Committee and is therefore also involved in the endangered-species issue, suggests that Culver call Nelson. There is always a possibility that a senator is not as enthusiastic as his staff is about pursuing a certain course, and the only way to find out is to talk to the senator directly. (Members of the Administration have made the same point to me.) Culver wonders aloud if his calling Nelson might suggest that he is worried that his own side is not so strong, and he asks whether certain senators—Muskie; John Chafee, Republican of Rhode Island; and Robert Stafford, Republican of Vermont—all of whom are strong environmentalists and members of the Environment and Public Works Committee, might be expected to stay with him or go with Nelson. Their defection could be very damaging to Culver. He considers the fact that Nelson's opposition "puts us in the middle ground," and says that that might not be so bad, but he also worries that if Nelson does move to kill Culver's proposal the environmentalists will have to support Nelson. "What do you think, Dick?" he asks Oshlo. "Should we just let this run its course?" Oshlo suggests that Culver will have to be prepared to "take a little heat" from the environmentalists but that he doesn't think a vote on such a move by Nelson will be severely damaging to Culver. He says that they must make sure that the other senators' offices understand what the issue is really about. "I'm not sure it's any big deal," Culver says. "It's just a little surprising to me." Clearly, he is uncomfortable with the new complications. Then he says, referring to the Nelson and Stennis positions, "I'm not sure that when we get to a conference with the House we won't be politically stronger if we've had the votes on both sides of us. It might be a little difficult in the short run, but it might add some starch for later."

He reaches Nelson on the phone, and becomes jocular and expansive when he talks to him. "Gaylord! How you doin'? How you been?" He laughs at something Nelson has said. "I missed you in Alaska, Gaylord. You should have gone." He talks a little about the trip, and then says, "You got anything new for me? I've been away." He listens to Nelson for a few moments and then says loudly, in mock horror, "You're going to *what? Oppose* it?" He laughs. "Gaylord! You of all people! *Gaylord!* To me? Your buddy? Gaylord! I mean, a lot of guys around here want to have an issue rather than do something about a problem, but not you, Gaylord, not you."

He goes on, in good humor. He and Nelson are, after all, close friends, and, beyond that, a good bit of the negotiating, testing, that goes on in the Senate is done in the atmosphere—real or contrived—of good fellowship. Culver spent some time with Nelson when he made the speech to the Democratic Convention in Wisconsin in June. Now he says to him, "Remember we talked about this on that rowboat on that beautiful lake in Wisconsin, and we visited a little about this? Didn't I detect a nodding of the head? You see, Gaylord, you should have come to Alaska with us. You see, if you stay around here you get in trouble. I don't believe, Gaylord, you'd do this to your buddy. I just *know* you've been trying to reach me so that we can talk about some amendments we can work out mutually. I *know* that's what you have in mind." Culver's staff has told him that Nelson has some amendments to Culver's proposal, and that perhaps the announcement that he is going to oppose it is a bargaining position. Culver puffs on a cigar and listens to Nelson. He is sober now; Nelson apparently isn't backing down. "Well, I know that, sir—I'm very much aware of that," Culver says. "I really think this strengthens the act. I didn't know what you wanted to do—if you wanted to visit about some amendments." Then he laughs, and says, "Well, if you're just going to let me get bloodied in the cross fire while you're standing there in your white hat." He laughs at something Nelson says, and then hangs up.

"O.K.," he says to the staff. "Let's make sure we're ready." He continues, "We've got to get the best substantive rebuttal to the argument that there is no need to change the law. Nelson said that Tellico probably would not be exempted under our proposal, and I agreed with him, but it's best not to get into that on the floor if it can be avoided. We have to know about every project that's backed up because of legal difficulties and which state it's in." He clearly doesn't like having been taken by surprise.

After the staff leaves, he says to me, "This is just a new difficulty, after we took some heat for proposing to change the law in the first place. And it comes just when people were beginning to calm down and support our proposal. Now the environmentalists are going to have to oppose me. Now we might lose some of the senators we've worked so long to hold. I don't know how many votes we can hold." He suggests that his staff is being optimistic.

The Senate stops working shortly before six tonight without having taken any votes. A number of senators are going to the White House for a briefing on foreign policy. (Culver attended one three weeks ago.) Culver's wife and their two younger children are at their home in McGregor. The other two children, teen-age daughters, are staying with friends in Washington, and the Culvers have rented out their Washington home for the summer. Almost as an afterthought, Culver has arranged to stay with Charles Stevenson tonight. He hasn't had time to figure out where he will stay for the rest of the summer. Right now, all he can think about is getting some sleep.

3

TUESDAY, JULY 11TH: At nine-thirty, on the way to Room 4200 of the Dirksen Senate Office Building for the hearing on the National Environmental Policy Act, Culver tells me that he has had a good night's sleep and feels better. This morning, as usual, he reached his office at eight-thirty. The Senate began meeting at nine o'clock, but no votes are expected before eleven. Culver hopes to have his hearing over before then and get back to his office to prepare for offering his amendment to the military-procurement bill stipulating that the new giant nuclear carrier provided for in the bill should be the last large carrier of any kind.

At the hearing, Culver reads an opening statement that his staff has prepared for him. The hearing room is filled—such is the interest in this issue—but for the moment Culver is the only senator present. He spells out the trade-offs: the concern of business that a requirement for statements on the environmental impact of products for which export loans have been made by the Export-Import Bank will put American manufacturers at a competitive disadvantage against those of other nations, as opposed to the arguments of those who feel that "we have a responsibility to be aware of the impact of our federal actions on the world ecology, in order to avoid exporting our environmental misfortunes abroad." He mentions specifically the export of chemicals that are banned or strictly regulated within the United States.

Herbert Hansell, the legal adviser to the State Department, testifies. He is accompanied by the chairman of the Council on Environmental Quality and the chairman of the Export-Import Bank. Hansell tells Culver what he already knows: that the Administration is discussing a response to the Stevenson amendment, and—using the kind of language which Administration officials, and especially, it seems, those from the State Department, often use when they testify, and which tries the patience of even the more patient members of Congress—that the government agencies "are making substantial progress in developing a practical approach to achieve this objective." He continues, "A number of details need to be worked out, and other agencies need to be consulted, but we see the basis of agreement that can be recommended to the President shortly." As the State Department witness testifies, Senator Malcolm Wallop, Republican of Wyoming and the ranking minority member of the subcommittee, shows up. Kathi Korpon is sitting beside Culver, and George Jacobson is behind them. From time to time, Culver confers with his aides.

When Hansell finishes, Culver says, "I am a little disappointed that we don't have an approved Administration recommendation at this time." He reminds the witnesses that he has already granted the Administration one delay, and, bit by bit, his impatience spills out. "We wait and wait for this Administration to, it seems to me, get its act together in a number of different policy areas," he says. "You have a four-year term, as far as I read the Constitution."

Then comes sarcasm: "You want me to go to bat in stopping Senator Stevenson from going ahead with this particular approach. How would you like to be me or Senator Wallop and go to Senator Stevenson and say, 'Senator Stevenson, with regard to that Export-Import matter, please be advised that'—in your own words—'we see the basis of agreement that can be recommended to the President shortly.' That ought to overwhelm him, don't you think?" Then, his voice getting stronger, he plows through the statement he has just been hearing, reading back portions of it in a mocking tone. His annoyance appears to be real. Culver can sometimes get huffy in a hearing for no great reason, but today his pique seems justified. The Administration has asked for his help, and he has obliged, and now these witnesses are coming before him unprepared; moreover, they are taking his time when he has a great many other things to do. He gets increasingly worked up, and says, "Then you say on page 6, 'This program may be included in an executive order.' May be. Are you just going to send out a press release? Is it going to be an executive order? Are you going to submit legislation? I really think, with all due respect, it is awfully hard to carry water in a bucket that has so many holes you can't get away from the well before it is empty." He asks some specific questions about how the new policy might work, and gets vague answers.

Now his annoyance is total. "We aren't having this hearing to hear from you that if and when you can ever have a meeting with the President of the United States you are going to tell him what you intend to do," he says. "Because the next time you say, 'Senator, would you please have another meeting'—you know, I am awfully busy, too. If you can tell me what you have got in mind here on this one occasion that I have an opportunity to seriously focus on this subject, I am here to entertain that. . . . Have you got anything to tell me? Otherwise, I am not interested in talking to my friend Senator Stevenson about it; it is too embarrassing. Senator Stevenson would say, 'Well, what is going to happen?' 'Well, I just talked to this nice man Mr. Hansell. He is going to talk to the President and tell him about timing and flexibility and contents. Just take my word, Adlai.' I am not going to play that role for you. . . . Make your case. And the case can't be 'If and when we get the ear of the President, we may have a policy.' Tell me something at least substantively. We don't need any more mood music about how complicated it is."

The hearing goes on in that vein, with Culver asking precise questions and then expressing annoyance with the answers. As it proceeds, Senator Muskie arrives. He asks Mrs. Korpon to get him a cup of coffee, and she does. Culver concludes with instructions to the witnesses to come up with a policy that assumes the United States has an obligation to protect the world environment and that protects the third world from the misapplication of technology.

At eleven-forty, Culver recesses the hearing and races over to the Senate floor. The buzzers have sounded, signalling a roll-call vote, and he hasn't had time to get back to his office to prepare for the debate on his aircraft-carrier amendment. Senators have fifteen minutes to get to the floor to vote once the buzzers have sounded. As they rush from place to place, they carry cards in their pockets listing their schedules for the day; usually the lists are very long, and often they become theoretical.

While Culver is on the Senate floor, he talks with Stennis—who, as chairman of the Armed Services Committee, is managing the military-procurement bill—about the timing and also the substance of his aircraft-carrier amendment. Culver asks Stennis his position on the amendment, and Stennis says that he hasn't decided yet but that he has some problems with it. Culver asks what they are. Stennis tells him he is concerned that it would place restraints on the President. Culver suggests that the two men's staffs try to work something out. He leaves the implication that otherwise there will be a floor fight on this, or perhaps even a proposal by someone else to knock out the carrier provided for in the bill—a possibility Stennis is concerned about. Even though such an amendment is unlikely to carry, managers of bills have to worry about what might happen in an emotional moment. Culver's staff is also negotiating on his behalf with the staff of Senator Dewey Bartlett, Republican of Oklahoma, about an amendment concerning American military equipment stored in Europe. Culver confers off the Senate floor with Charles Stevenson about these negotiations, and with George Jacobson about a problem that has arisen over the ground rules for the debate on the endangered-species bill.

The Senate floor debates proceed largely by unanimous-consent agreements among the senators: on how many hours will be allowed for general debate on a bill; on how much time will be allowed for each amendment; and even on such minor questions as whether certain staff aides can be on the Senate floor during debates. This morning, Culver learned that Nelson has asked for more time for consideration of his amendment, and that Malcolm Wallop, who, as the ranking Republican on Culver's Resource Protection Subcommittee, will manage the bill with Culver, is likely to object. Culver is worried that if Nelson is given more time the unanimous-consent agreement on the endangered-species bill could come undone, and he has told George Jacobson to tell an assistant to Majority Leader Byrd that if an exception to the unanimous-consent agreement that has already been reached on the bill is made for Nelson, others will also want more time.

At twelve-thirty, Culver goes to a luncheon in the office of Alan Cranston, of California, the Democratic Whip, to discuss SALT. A group of about seventeen senators now meet for lunch every two weeks to consider this topic. This group grew out of a meeting of a few senators and Administration officials which was held at Culver's house last November. The idea, Culver has told me, was to organize a group that would become well informed and be in a position to conduct a strong debate on behalf of a SALT agreement and to help the Administration, whose competence to handle the issue was in doubt, prepare for a SALT fight. Gradually, the group grew. Before the Fourth of July recess, it met with Harold Brown, the Secretary of Defense. Today's lunch is interrupted from time to time for roll-call votes on the defense bill. When Culver comes into the Senate chamber to vote, he checks with Charles Stevenson on the progress of his negotiations.

Over lunch in the Senate dining room, another senator talks to me about the frustrations of the job. "It's the pressures," he says. "The pressures of the institution. You've got to be at a committee meeting, you've got to be on the floor, you've got to do this, you've got to do that, you've got to be back in your state, you've got to go to a reception here. After a while, you say, 'Wait a minute. Do I have to do all this?' The staff all want to be close to the boss, and they all want to sit down and talk to you about what they're working on, and you don't have time, but if you don't talk to them you create a morale problem. It's hard to put up with a lot of the baloney around here—the posturing. A lot of guys up here are robots. They just go around making speeches and shaking hands and voting politically. They don't concentrate on the legislation or take any chances. And people treat you like a pincushion. I don't mean the constituents—they're your boss—but, no matter how busy or preoccupied you are, anyone feels he can come up and ask you a question or argue with you about something. It's as if you're fair game at any hour. There's no peace, and very little time to think."

At today's SALT luncheon, the senators were assigned specific subjects in which they were to develop expertise so as to be able to handle them during the debate. Culver, along with four other senators, was given the largest subject: the United States-Soviet strategic balance. Now Culver, who has returned to the Senate floor for a vote, chats with Dick Clark for a while about how his race for reëlection this year is going. Culver's friend Paul Sarbanes, Democrat of Maryland, comes over to him and gives him a packet of material concerning the Administration's proposal to lift the embargo on the sale of arms to Turkey—a move that Sarbanes opposes. Culver talks with Birch Bayh, Democrat of Indiana, about a problem in the administration of juvenile-delinquency programs.

When the senators are summoned to the floor for a vote, they get one of their rare chances to see each other, to trade information, to transact business. Senators, stretched thin on a number of committees (House members serve on fewer of them), trailed about by aides (few House members are trailed by aides), on call to more constituents and sought out by more government officials than House members are, do not see nearly as much of each other as their counterparts in the House do. They lead far more autonomous lives.

Culver, a gregarious type and a man who also understands the importance of good relationships with his colleagues in accomplishing things—of the purposeful conviviality that marks Capitol Hill—

gets around this problem as best he can by spending time in the senators' few gathering places: in the cloakroom behind the Senate floor; in the gym; in the senators' private dining room (actually two rooms with an open door between them, one containing a big round table for Democrats, the other a similar table for Republicans); and in the office of Stanley Kimmitt, the Secretary of the Senate, where at the end of the day an odd assortment of Democrats—among them, James O. Eastland, of Mississippi; Warren Magnuson, of Washington; Nelson and Culver—plus an occasional Republican or two, may gather to drink and talk. (Culver himself does not drink. He used to, but liquor and the temper were not a good combination—early in his House career, he got into a minor scrape with police—and eight years ago he simply stopped.) Culver classifies himself as a liberal, but he does not have the arrogant, or snobbish, quality that some liberals have, and he gets on well with Democratic and Republican conservatives. Culver also goes over to the House gym on occasion. He stays in touch with his former House colleagues, apparently not only because he enjoys the relatively less pretentious House members and shares their outlook on many things but also because it helps him know what is going on in the House, and to get things done. Not many senators bother to maintain allies in the House, people who can help them with their legislation there. When Culver was in the House, he managed to get close to its leadership, and formed friendships with his contemporaries and also went on hunting trips with some of the older and more powerful Southerners. "He's interesting that way," an associate of Culver's says. "He's not at all establishmentarian in thought, but he likes to be with the established centers of power. He cultivates the powers that be by his company and good fellowship but not by his vote."

Now Culver, back on the floor, is talking again to Stennis about the timing and substance of his amendment. Stennis wants Culver's amendment to come up by midafternoon. The amendment says that all future requests for aircraft carriers shall be for carriers smaller than the current giant ones "unless and until the President has fully advised the Congress that construction of such ships is not in the national interest." In order to get Stennis to go along with his amendment, Culver agrees to a minor change, making it clear that it does not apply to the carrier in the bill. With that, Culver approaches Barry Goldwater, a member of the Armed Services Committee, who has expressed reservations about the continued deployment of large carriers, and asks him to speak in behalf of his amendment. Goldwater declines, saying that he will support it but not speak in its favor. Culver tells him that Stennis is going to announce his acceptance of the amendment, and Goldwater then agrees to speak in its behalf. Culver figures that when the amendment is taken up in conference with the House it will help to have had Goldwater for it.

While all this has been going on, Culver has had to give his attention to other matters, too. At about three-thirty, he attended a brief meeting of the Democratic caucus to ratify some new committee assignments, including that of Mrs. Maryon Allen, the widow of James Allen, who died in June, to the Senate Judiciary Committee. His office has sent over some material on endangered species for him to put in the *Congressional Record.* An interview he was to give to an Iowa reporter on the subject this afternoon had to be postponed. His office has sent him a note saying that he has been asked to appear on "Good Morning, America" tomorrow, along with a number of other senators, to discuss SALT and the Soviet trials. Culver declines; he doesn't think that that is a very good forum for discussing such a complicated issue. (He turns down many requests for television interviews.) He receives a memo from Don Brownlee telling him that all three Cedar Rapids/Waterloo television stations and also the Cedar Rapids *Gazette* carried stories the previous day about the fact that the Rath Packing Company, whose headquarters are in Waterloo and which has been having economic difficulties, had, with Culver's help, been awarded a ninety-six-thousand-nine-hundred-dollar contract to provide the Defense Department with bacon. He talks to Wallop about the question of time for debate on the endangered-species bill. He leaves the floor to take a call in the cloakroom from a personal friend and, later, a call from Kennedy about whether he plans to go to the softball game tonight. Kennedy says that he will go if Culver does. Actually, there is some question whether the Senate will adjourn in time for either of them to make it. Culver works at his desk—next to an aisle, in the last of four rows on the Democratic side, which is on the left as the senators face the presiding officer—reading his notes for his forthcoming speech on his amendment and showing the amendment to some of his colleagues. He ducks out to a room off the Senate floor to work on his speech, and after a short time Charles Stevenson, a quiet young man with dark-blond hair, a mustache, and rimless glasses, comes and tells him that the amendment will be brought up shortly.

At a little after four, Culver is recognized to offer his amendment. He stands at his desk and, as he explains the amendment, slowly paces three or four steps back and forth in different directions from his desk, as if within an invisible circle. Unlike most senators, he does not use a lapel microphone to amplify his voice. He does not need one. And, as is his habit, he speaks extemporaneously, referring only occasionally to the notes on his desk. This is a technique he has long since developed; he is aware that when a senator makes a speech he is far more likely to command the attention and respect of his colleagues if he seems to actually know what he is talking about, and that the best way to create that impression is to be prepared and to speak extemporaneously, rather than to read a speech in a manner that suggests that it was written by one's staff. Charles Stevenson has given Culver "talking points," and Culver has been reworking them and making his own notes, and now he just lets go.

As is his wont when he is making a point in debate, he repeats for emphasis: "In the past two years that I have had the opportunity to look in some detail at some of the current Navy programs . . . we have received, believe it or not, some six different five-year shipbuilding plans for the U.S. Navy. Six separate, distinct, and different submissions as to where the U.S. Navy is going to go in the next five years. In the last two years, we have received *six different proposals.*" He goes on to say that the Navy represents "the most significant area of current disarray within our over-all military force posture." His voice rising, he asks rhetorical questions about the role of the Navy: "What is its mission? Is its mission sea control? Is its mission to project force ashore?" And so on. As he speaks, sometimes his left hand chops the air, sometimes his right hand goes out in front of him, sometimes he spreads his arms and waves them up and down. "The role of the giant aircraft carrier in the world today is over," he says. He has the attention of the dozen or so senators who are present. (Not all senators are listened to when they speak.) He says, "You're talking about a forty-billion-dollar cost" for each carrier task force (the carrier plus its accompanying ships and planes) over its life cycle. The estimated cost of the new carrier itself is about two billion dollars. He says, "Anyone who thinks for a moment that the Soviet Union does not know, at this very moment, where each of our current fleet of aircraft carriers is does not know the first thing about military planning." Stennis comes over and sits three chairs away from Culver, watching him, nodding on occasion at this young man with whom he has suddenly found himself in agreement. Culver talks in a very loud voice now, as if he were in a ferocious argument. Some senators just get up and talk; some give formal speeches; Culver speaks forcefully, as if in strong debate, as if what he does in these few minutes will make all the difference. It doesn't seem to matter that he is clearly going to win on this issue; Culver is not given to doing things part-way. He has sometimes drawn a parallel between how he feels giving a speech and how he felt playing football.

"Mr. President," Culver says, "some of us have serious reservations about the wisdom in our national-security interests for a cost-effective over-all defense system of spending money in this bill for one more highly vulnerable nuclear aircraft carrier . . . because you can shoot it like a duck in a pond with highly accurate, precision-guided missiles." He repeats, incredulously, the cost—"a cost of forty billion dollars over the life cycle of that one task force." He is speaking passionately now. His face is red. His big voice fills the chamber. "If we are going to accept that judgment," and he repeats, "if we are going to accept that judgment," and then goes on, "this is one senator, this is one senator who is only going to do so if there is an agreement by the Senate and the Congress that this is the last one." Culver says, "This is one time that maybe we can get out ahead of the curve." This is a theme that runs through much of what he does. "Mr. President," he concludes, after speaking for about fifteen minutes, "in my judgment we now have an opportunity that we never seem to grasp. We now have an opportunity to close the books on a fading era and to enhance our naval power in the future by adopting this amendment, and I would urge its adoption."

John Tower, Republican of Texas and also a member of the Armed Services Committee, engages Culver in a colloquy that establishes that the amendment would allow the President some discretion to recommend another large carrier, but only if he justifies such a decision to Congress.

Stennis praises Culver's speech. "The Senator from Iowa has made a masterful speech," he says. Even if one allows for the usual flattery that senators bestow on each other, it seems that Stennis is impressed. "He has made a fine presentation here concerning a major problem," Stennis says. "His influence is vast." Culver watches Stennis intently. Stennis points out that the amendment does not affect the carrier provided for in the bill, and says that he will accept it.

John Chafee, who was Secretary of the Navy in the Nixon Administration, and who is a friend of Culver's, speaks on behalf of Culver's amendment, as does Dale Bumpers, a progressive Democrat from Arkansas, who used to serve on the Armed Services Committee with Culver and often sided with him, and who is a member of the SALT group.

And Barry Goldwater speaks for Culver's amendment. "I think that the day of the carrier has passed," Goldwater says, and he points out that for the amount of money a carrier costs, one could buy a lot of B-1 bombers. Goldwater apparently hasn't given up on the B-1 bomber. Culver has stitched together an interesting coalition.

The amendment is easily agreed to by voice vote. Culver does not ask for a roll call. His theory is that by having the amendment agreed to by voice vote he can argue in conference with the House that it was not even controversial—that even Tower and Goldwater were on the floor and hardly any objection was raised. That is more helpful, he feels, than having a roll-call vote, on which some thirty or forty senators might feel constrained to go on record against him.

Off the Senate floor, Don Brownlee is waiting for Culver to approve a press release on the Senate's adoption of his amendment. Culver comes off the floor and makes a minor correction in the release. Steve Rapp, the staff director of Culver's Juvenile Delinquency Subcommittee, is also waiting for him. He wants to talk to Culver about the Administration's efforts to arrive at a plan to reorganize the various agencies that deal with inspecting the Mexican border for the importation of drugs. Rapp tells Culver that he has learned from a contact within the Administration that it now seems that the President will not send up the reorganization tomorrow, as had been planned, because "the special interests" are opposed; and he urges Culver to call the White House to urge that the plan be sent up. Culver asks, "Why would a call from me make a bit of difference?" He points out that his subcommittee does not have jurisdiction over reorganization plans. Rapp says that the White House tends to hear more from the special interests opposed to reorganization plans than from the people who are for them. "It's a mess and long overdue," Culver agrees, "but I can't see why a call from me would matter." He says to Rapp, "Tell your contacts down there that you talked to me and I want to see what they're proposing, and you might also tell them that for an Administration that came in with a pledge to thoroughly reorganize the government they have a long way to go."

Culver goes back to the floor to agree with Bartlett's new version of the amendment on American equipment in Europe. On the floor, he talks with George Jacobson about a "Dear Colleague" letter—the kind of letter that senators send around to their colleagues explaining their bills and amendments—on the endangered-species bill. He talks with some senators about when the endangered-species bill will come up; there was some possibility that it would be brought up on Friday, when Culver was planning to be in Iowa, but now it appears that it will come up on Monday. After he leaves the floor, he tells me about the timing on the endangered-species bill. I ask him how he will be able to jump right into managing a complicated bill immediately after returning from Iowa. "We're always getting back from someplace and getting right into something," he says.

Culver and I sit in the Senate dining room while he has a cup of coffee and reviews the events of the day, and, as he sometimes likes to do when he unwinds, he muses about politics and the Senate. It is now about six o'clock, and he has to wait for further roll-call votes. He says, "Let's visit for a while." He talks about life in the Senate. "Isn't this just crazy?" he asks. "It's gradually become so frenetic and intensified. Actually, today was a relatively easy day. Often, there are more meetings, and more constituents to see. We're spread so thin and we're on too many committees, and the circuits are overloaded—even though I'm one of those who have tried to pick a few things to do and do those well. Even if you do that—even if you do the things that are hit to your field—frankly, if I were to do any one to my satisfaction I could spend full time on it and still not feel in total command. But at least then you wouldn't feel the frustration of jumping around a lot. The trade-off is you have the excitement of a number of stimuli." He continues, "Another thing that's interesting is what the psychic needs are. I think anyone who seeks public office has some need for gratification or approval that affords the energy and the presumption to aspire to it.

I think after you've served a few times, or run a few times, you begin to wonder how much you want to keep doing it. Part of it is that at a certain point in your life you look at how much you've accomplished and how much time you have left. Just as people who have done other things think of doing something else, I think people who have done this—if they have things in a healthy balance—ask themselves how long they want to do this. I think actually it's important to have that attitude starting out: that you know you can do something else, that the world isn't going to come to an end if you're not reëlected. It's important to keep that at the ready when you win and when you function here."

As we are talking, another senator wanders into the dining room, and Culver greets him: "How you doin'?"

The senator pauses, smiles, and says, "I don't know whether to whistle or tie my shoes."

Culver laughs. "Join the crowd," he says.

We talk about Culver's speech today. He says, "In politics, you can give a good speech, hit it right—the juices are flowing, and you know you're doing it well, and you have a high. And yet you know—if you're your own worst critic, if you're healthy—that the next time you can bomb out. It's not dissimilar from a football game. You can know you did well then and yet know that another time you won't. But that apprehension is healthy, and you shouldn't lose it. In each event, you have to try to do your best. Each time, you think of what you should have said. To that extent, it's unrelenting." (Culver is known among his friends for questioning them, and himself, after a speech or some other public action, about how he did. "Did I go on too long?" "Did I hit him too hard?") "It's part of the challenge," he says. "In that way, it's like competitive sports—you admire a guy who's playing hard and fair. Around here, you admire someone who works from views and works hard and advocates effectively." In private conversations, Culver can be quite explicit about whom he admires and whom he does not. He clearly does not admire posturers or those who he feels sell out their principles—or don't have any—or those who are, in his eyes, lazy, or those who mean well but are ineffective. Culver's objectivity about himself and his ability to see things for what they are can be a burden. Most politicians who posture don't seem to have difficulty doing it. Most are able to justify a vote on the ground that otherwise it would "be too difficult to explain." One theory about the design of our political system is that the Senate, whose members have to run for reëlection every six years—as opposed to the House, whose members have to run every two years—is more immune to the passions of the moment and therefore less "political." More than one senator, citing the increasing number of votes on, and in favor of, emotion-laden proposals, has said to me that this theory is not borne out. Culver says, "Sometimes we go in there and act like a vacuum cleaner for every frustration from that morning's papers."

At seven-forty-five, the Senate takes its final vote on the military-procurement bill. After Culver votes, he phones an Iowa radio station that wanted to talk to him about his aircraft-carrier amendment, then he and I run down the Senate steps and join Kennedy in Kennedy's car, a blue convertible, to go to the softball game. On the way to the game, Kennedy teases Culver, telling me that actually Culver has never played in a softball game before; that actually Culver is an entirely different person from the one I have been seeing in the past two days. They joke about something that happened in the Senate recently. The two men clearly amuse each other, and have a string of running jokes.

The softball game is in the Ellipse, the large

park behind the White House. The two senators (Clark is not here) have not had a chance to change out of their suits. The sun is setting now, and it is a cool evening with a soft breeze. The Kennedy team wears green-and-white T-shirts with "Boston Ted Sox" printed on them; the Culver-and-Clark team wears black T-shirts imprinted with the senators' names in gold and a gold corncob. The staffs cheer when the senators turn up; it gives them a lift. They usually turn up only when the team of one of their close friends is playing. The score is tied, and the game has gone into extra innings.

To the delight of the staffs, Kennedy steps up to bat, and Culver thereupon insists on pitching. "Overhand or underhand?" Culver yells. He pitches one (underhand) that goes way over Kennedy's head.

"Ball one!" Kennedy shouts. (There is no umpire.)

"How did you call that?" Culver asks in mock incredulity. He gets the pitching under control and sends a few over the plate. Kennedy lets them go by. "Let's go down swinging, Ted," Culver shouts. Another goes by Kennedy. *"Will you take a cut at it?"* Culver yells to Kennedy. Kennedy is smiling. Finally, Kennedy hits a single, and someone on his team scores. Culver cheers lustily when Kennedy is later tossed out at third.

Culver is first up to bat for his side. Kennedy plays center field. Culver waves him back and points, like Babe Ruth pointing to the bleachers. Then he hits a tiny bunt and runs swiftly—surprisingly swiftly for someone of his bulk—to first base. Later, he makes it to second, and then to third, on fielding mistakes, and then, after a fly ball is caught, he scores.

Although Culver does not get much exercise now, the athlete in him is still visible. He and Kennedy are only in part putting on a show for their staffs; they are also caught up in a combination of their own competitive instincts—like other grown men when they get out on a softball field—and amusement at each other. The game goes on for a while: Culver gets a hit into center field (at this point, Kennedy is pitching), and the Iowans lead, but when the Kennedy team bats again Kennedy gets a single, then slides into second, and eventually they stop with the score nine to eight, Kennedy. By this time, there is a major but good-humored dispute between the two teams over exactly how many extra innings had been agreed to ("You wouldn't be proud of this, Ted," Culver says as indignantly as he can) and exactly who won. Each senator poses for pictures with his team and leads it in a cheer for the other. "Let's get out a press release," Kennedy suggests to his team.

4

WEDNESDAY, JULY 12TH: The Senate went into session at eight o'clock this morning on another military bill, this one for construction of military buildings, and so on, as opposed to the "hardware" authorized in yesterday's military-procurement bill. By now, at ten-thirty, Culver has met on the Senate steps with a 4-H Club delegation from Council Bluffs, posed for pictures with them, and given them a brief tour of the Capitol, telling its history and describing the fresco under the dome in some detail; gone, along with Clark, to the Russell Office Building to make a statement introducing the director of the Iowa Department of Transportation's Railroad Division to the Surface Transportation Subcommittee of the Senate Commerce Committee, before which the director was to testify (Culver says that he does this sort of thing about a half-dozen times a year); posed for pictures with two young women who are representing Iowa at Girls Nation, an American Legion program (they were supposed to meet Culver on the Senate steps, but were late, and finally caught up with him at the subcommittee hearing). Now he is heading for a meeting of the Judiciary Committee, in the Dirksen Building.

As Culver moves through the halls, his size makes him appear to be lumbering along, but actually he covers a lot of ground quickly. While he makes his way to the Judiciary Committee meeting, he is briefed by Josy Gittler, a petite, dark-haired woman who is the chief counsel of Culver's Juvenile Delinquency Subcommittee. (She was the first woman law professor at the University of Iowa.) Yesterday, Miss Gittler gave Culver memorandums on the bills that are to come up before the committee, for him to read last night, and now she briefs him on them: a bill to give the Attorney General the right to sue, and intervene in suits, on behalf of persons who are in state institutions and whose rights have allegedly been violated (she tells him that the vote will be very close, and that Birch Bayh, who is sponsoring the proposal, and the Justice Department are very anxious to have him there, and then she reports how various members of the committee are expected to vote), and measures concerning bankruptcy laws and off-track betting.

Room 2300, where the Judiciary Committee is meeting, is a small room; the senators sit at a long table, and aides and officials and whatever onlookers have managed to get in stand against the walls. Eastland, the chairman, is at one end of the table. The committee is made up of a number of very liberal Democrats and very conservative Republicans and includes a couple of somewhat eccentric types, and the meetings are often lively and sometimes nearly chaotic. As the deliberations proceed, Culver studies the memorandums. These are other people's bills, and he will take no major role; what he wants to do here is understand as best he can what he is voting on. When bills or amendments are offered in the committee by someone whose views he generally shares, and whom he trusts, his inclination will be to go along, but still he wants to be sure of what he's doing. Paul Laxalt, Republican of Nevada, asks that consideration of Bayh's bill be postponed, because Strom Thurmond, Republican of South Carolina, is occupied on the Senate floor with the military-construction bill and has asked for a deferral. (Any senator can block a committee meeting when the Senate is in session.) Laxalt is a pleasant man, liked by his colleagues, and he makes the request in a reasonable tone. Bayh, who has struggled to get enough senators here who back his bill, says, "My problem is, Paul, everyone around this table is busier than a one-armed paperhanger, yet they have squeezed time to be here today." William Scott, a conservative Republican from Virginia, who has the reputation of being a rather limited man, and unpredictable, remarks that Thurmond is a retired general and therefore it's important for him to be on the floor. Culver says, "How about a retired member of the Marine Corps? I'm here."

The senators put the Bayh bill aside, and go on to take up two bankruptcy-law bills and some amendments to one of them, and pass them, and then they take up a bill dealing with interstate regulation of off-track betting. It is sponsored by Senator Charles McC. Mathias, a moderate Republican from Maryland, who is a well-liked man, and who usually lines up with the liberal Democrats on the committee. But Howard Metzenbaum, Democrat of Ohio, has some problems with the bill and asks that consideration of it, too, be postponed. Culver joins him in the request. Culver would like to know more about the implications of the bill. "Let's put it over, Mac, just so we can study it more," he says quietly. Mathias agrees. So these busy people have just given themselves another meeting to attend, more work to do. Dennis DeConcini, Democrat of Arizona, brings up Senate Joint Resolution 135, designating a weekend in late April as Days of Remembrance of Victims of the Holocaust. Eastland asks if there is any objection, and the committee quickly approves the resolution. After the meeting, Culver asks Miss Gittler to take another look at the off-track betting bill, and he goes back to his office to go over the schedule for his trip to Iowa this weekend. No Senate votes are scheduled before one o'clock.

In his office, Culver scans the press clippings and the news summary from the Iowa papers that Don Brownlee prepares for him each day. Culver is pleased that the Des Moines *Register* is running a two-part series explaining why the Endangered Species Act needs to be amended, and that this morning's Washington *Post* has an editorial supporting his approach. Earlier this morning, he asked his staff to prepare a statement for him to insert in the *Congressional Record* about the retirement of a political reporter for the Davenport-area *Quad-City Times*. Next, Culver looks over the notice sent out by the Democratic Whip about what is supposed to come up this week. He has been told that it is still possible that the endangered-species bill will come up Friday, and therefore he doesn't know whether he can be in Iowa then, as he had planned. At the other end, he is scheduled to return from Iowa—via Chicago, where he is to make a speech—about three o'clock on Monday. Dick Oshlo tells him that some of the staff have met with Nelson's staff, and it now seems that Nelson may not actually move to kill Culver's proposal but may simply engage in a colloquy with him on it and then offer some "perfecting amendments." Culver is pleased by this news. He goes over the various possibilities for the schedule in Iowa with Jim Larew, his appointments secretary. Larew, who is twenty-four, worked in Culver's 1974 Senate campaign as a field organizer, and in 1977 received a summa cum laude from Harvard for an honors thesis he wrote on the history of the Democratic Party in Iowa.

Culver goes into the scheduling in great detail—dealing with it as methodically as he deals with legislation: where each event will take place, what the possibility is for television coverage for each one, how many events can be worked in. He is not satisfied with an event that has been tentatively planned for Cedar Rapids, and asks Larew to come up with a better one. He considers whether he can go to a certain city and see just one group without offending others, and decides that he can't, and will go to that city on another trip, when he will have more time to spend there. Culver had been considering going to the Rath packing plant, but he won't be able to get to Waterloo until Saturday and the plant will be closed, so that is out. He decides to go instead to an armed-services recruiting center in Waterloo and talk with the recruiters about how they are coming in meeting their quotas for the volunteer service. "Get representatives of all the services there," he says. "Saturday afternoon is Sleepy Hollow for the media; we should give them notice of this event well in advance—it's a good, substantive story. I'll make a statement on the status of the volunteer services. Let's try to encourage as much interest in the Waterloo-area media as we can, and I think it's a suitable story for the wires out of Des Moines."

The fact that many senators can't get to their states except on weekends without missing votes—and they even take chances if they are gone on Fridays or Mondays—is a problem: it is hard to gather people for political events or for tours of facilities, or even to interest much of the local press, on a weekend. It's difficult to understand how these people can go as hard as they do during the week and then virtually campaign on the weekend, but they are expected to. There is an insatiability in the demands made on them by constituents, by staff, and by others who can get at them in Washington.

Culver tries to make an average of one working weekend trip to Iowa a month, and he is under some criticism in the state for not doing it more often. (Clark, by contrast, spends a great deal of time in the state. Culver and Clark, while they are friends and have similar—though not identical—voting records, have different temperaments and different political strengths and styles.) Culver rarely goes back to Iowa during the week for an event—a trip would take a lot of time out of his Senate schedule. He keeps up with what is happening within the Party in the state, but he doesn't find petty intra-Party squabbles interesting, and he thinks it is more important to do his work in Washington than to take the twenty-four hours or so it requires to attend one more midweek meeting of some club or other in the state. Senators whose states are nearer to Washington can, of course, get back and forth more easily. New York's senators, for example, virtually have offices on the shuttle. Senators are expected to be both in Washington and in their states, and little consideration seems to be given to the fact that they might also want to spend some time with their families, and to be whole people. Culver does take a great interest in his family and does want to live like a normal human being at least a certain amount of the time. Each senator has limits on what he can do without losing his dignity—or sanity. Culver establishes real human connections to a greater degree than most people in public life; it is clear that he genuinely likes people (some politicians, oddly, don't), and he is interested in what is happening in his friends' lives. He also reads books. The relentless and conflicting demands are what turn many Washington politicians into driven, machinelike people—if they were not that way before they got here—and are a large part of what destroys many families. But it doesn't make news when a senator reads a book, spends time with his family, or sits around talking with friends. There are no votes in doing those things, and it takes some strength, and some inner wholeness, to resist the pressures to almost never do them.

Today, Culver will have lunch in the Democratic senators' dining room. "It's one of the few opportunities, if any, around here to be in a genuinely relaxed and social setting with other senators," he says. "It gives us a chance to talk about what's going on in committees, on the floor, to trade rumors or scuttlebutt, or to talk about sports, about what went on at a party the night before." Some members hardly ever eat there. Some do quite frequently, among them Magnuson, Stennis, Nelson, Hollings, and Long. After lunch, Culver will preside over the Senate for an hour: a chore that—in the absence of the Vice President, who usually presides only when he might have to cast a tie-breaking vote—is rotated primarily among the more junior members of the Senate. Whoever presides is guided by the Parliamentarian if any complications arise.

After Culver gets back to his office this afternoon, things begin to pile up. He gives an interview to the reporter from Iowa who wants to talk to him about the endangered-species bill and whose appointment was postponed from yesterday. The interview takes longer than was scheduled; when Culver gets interested in a subject he keeps going. Several constituents have dropped by. Pat Sarcone, Culver's secretary, has been talking with the constituents, seeing if there's anything she can do to help them. The tone of a senator's office is often set by such a person. She must understand his needs and moods, protect him, and, at the same time, see that the right people do get through to him, and, also at the same time, be pleasant to callers and visitors. Some senators' secretaries become so protective as to cause their bosses problems with constituents and others. Miss Sarcone, who comes from a political family in Des Moines and has worked for Culver ever since he came to the Senate, understands her boss's temperament and handles the demands on him, and on herself, efficiently, perceptively, and with good humor.

When Culver finishes with the reporter, a half hour behind schedule, he drops into an outer office to greet two constituents—nuns from Clarke College, in Dubuque. "I'm afraid I'm running a little behind," he tells them. They thank him for writing in their behalf to some federal education officials, and he tells them he hopes to see them in Dubuque. A meeting with Phil Hilder, who has been a mail clerk on his staff and is leaving for law school in the fall, is postponed until tomorrow. Now Culver meets with two men—one of them used to be on his staff—who work for the Small Business Administration and are directors of a forthcoming White House conference and want to brief him on their plans. "Now, wait," Culver says to them as they explain their plan. "Why are you having regional conferences before you have state conferences?" It's late in the afternoon, and Culver is pressed, and tired, and he gets a bit cranky. The staff tries not to schedule many meetings for him after four o'clock, in order to give him time to be on the Senate floor, to get caught up on his work, to regroup, to see what needs to be done. Shortly after he begins talking to the S.B.A. men, the buzzers sound, indicating a roll-call vote. Culver buttons his collar, tightens his tie, and puts on his jacket to go over to the Senate floor.

On the way, he tells me that Mike Naylor, his legislative director, has just given him a memorandum asking him to make calls to Frank Moore, the President's assistant for congressional liaison, and to an official of the Office of Management and Budget about his proposal to provide a tax deduction for small businesses that insure themselves for product liability. Naylor has heard that a final decision is going to be made tomorrow about the Administration's position, and the rumor is that it is going to be contrary to Culver's proposal. Culver doesn't know whether the roll call will be on the military-construction bill or on an amendment to another bill: there were indications earlier that the Senate might set the military-construction bill aside temporarily to take up the other one. On the floor, Culver learns that the vote is on the Commodity Futures Trading Commission, and after he votes he chats with Dale Bumpers for a while about the Soviet trials and then goes out to the cloakroom to call Frank Moore. He tells Moore of his interest in the legislation, and says that he has received signals that the Administration's position is going to be adverse to his own, and asks him to call the O.M.B. official and relay his message. He suggests that Moore tell the O.M.B. official that he and Nelson, and also Representative Abner Mikva, Democrat of Illinois, have held hearings on the subject, and to consider that they might be in a position to oppose the Administration. Now, having learned that there will not be another vote for at least a half hour, he goes to the Senate gym for a swim, as he often does to get a break from the pressure. He tells me that he gets relief from the strain by going to the gym and kidding around with his colleagues. I have heard some senators and House members talk about literally hiding from their staff members by going to the gym.

At six-thirty, Culver returns to his office, looking refreshed. He has already been to the Senate floor for several votes. A staff member gives him some briefing material for a meeting tomorrow, and Culver asks him a number of questions. Sometimes when Culver is being briefed one can see that he is being told more than he wants to hear. He catches on quickly, but the staff, after all, is steeped in information and wants to pass it along. His eyes will start to fade out, and he will say, somewhat abruptly, to move the conversation along, "O.K. Anything else?" (The other side of this is that he does not like to have to explain something to a staff member more than once.) Culver has an unusually retentive mind, and it is not just one that can spew back what he has been told, or what he has read, but one that absorbs, generates questions, makes connections between things he knows. One of his Senate colleagues says, "Culver has a towering intellect and an inquisitive mind and is intellectually enormously demanding of himself and of associates. When he gets hold of an issue, he studies it, he reads it, he thinks it, he absorbs it." Now Culver talks with Dick Oshlo and Jim Larew about tomorrow's schedule, signs his mail, returns several phone calls, and makes arrangements to have his baggage transferred to the home of some old friends, where he will be staying.

Culver tells me, "What subcommittee you're on is often the luck of the draw. You might not be on it because you have a burning interest in the issue it's concerned with, and we are all spread too thin already. Then you get a bright staff person who works for months on something in the subcommittee that he's particularly interested in, and finally you don't want to disappoint him or her, and so you say 'Go ahead,' only to regret it later because you find yourself involved in something that you don't have sufficient interest in, and spending your energy and political capital on frustrating and unsatisfying efforts."

At seven-thirty, Culver and I join two of his close friends, Alan Baron and Jim Johnson, for dinner at the Palm, a steak restaurant where a number of political people like to eat. Baron is from Iowa, has been heavily involved in national politics, and publishes a political newsletter called *The Baron Report;* Johnson, who is from Minnesota and is executive assistant to Vice President Mondale, first met Culver when Johnson worked in Iowa, among other places, on Edmund Muskie's 1972 Presidential campaign, and then he spent a lot of time helping Culver with his campaign for the Senate two years later. Both Baron and Johnson are very intelligent and have a good sense of humor, and Culver enjoys their company and dines with them from time to time at the Palm. (Often, they are joined by John Reilly, another former Iowan, who is now a Washington attorney, but Reilly cannot make it this evening.) The conversation consists of political gossip, some serious talk about what has been happening, and a great many stories and jokes. As is usually the case in such situations, Culver's humor dominates. It ranges through quick reactions, one-liners, clowning, kidding and reactions to being kidded, and stories. Many of the stories are on himself, in what he recognizes are ludicrous or absurd situations. He gets wound up in the telling of stories; he feeds in little subjokes, puts a lot of energy, even his bulk, into it, laughing so hard himself, and usually repeating the punch line two or three times—interrupting with a "Huh?" and laughing harder each time—that one is swept along by the force as well as the substance. Culver has several laughs: sometimes his mouth turns up and he laughs silently, his big body shaking; sometimes he laughs aloud, at various decibel levels; sometimes he laughs so hard that he doubles over, holding his stomach with one arm.

5

THURSDAY, JULY 13TH: At nine-thirty, Culver is the only senator present in Room 424 of the Russell Office Building, a large green and marble room, for a meeting of his Juvenile Delinquency Subcommittee to mark up legislation to double the penalties for the illicit manufacture or distribution of PCP and to regulate the distribution of one of its ingredients—piperidine. This legislation is sponsored by Culver and Senator William Hathaway, Democrat of Maine, who, with Kennedy and Nelson, is among Culver's closest friends in the Senate. The bill is a substitute for one that was sponsored by Lloyd Bentsen, Democrat of Texas, and thirty-three other senators. Culver's subcommittee has jurisdiction over drug enforcement, and in June he and Hathaway, who heads a subcommittee dealing with drug abuse, held two days of hearings on the legislation. The hearings showed that PCP is used by about seven million people, and it is more potent than cocaine, that people who use it cannot distinguish between reality and unreality and lose sensation in their extremities, and that its use led to at least a hundred deaths last year. The subcommittee will also take up a proposal, sponsored by Senator Sam Nunn, Democrat of Georgia, that would permit the forfeiture of monetary or other proceeds from drug trafficking. Under current law, the government can seize, for example, an automobile or a boat in which illegal drugs are transported but not the proceeds from the drugs' sale. Before coming to the meeting room, Culver has gone over the subject matter with Steve Rapp.

After a while, Senators Mathias and Wallop, members of the subcommittee, arrive, providing a quorum, and at ten minutes to ten Culver calls the meeting to order. There are only two spectators. Steve Rapp sits behind Culver; a few other aides and a stenographer are present. The three senators proceed rather formally, because there is a record to be established for when this legislation is considered on the Senate floor. Culver carefully talks about PCP, about what the hearings showed, and about what is in the legislation pending before the subcommittee. Birch Bayh, who is a member of the subcommittee, and who has some amendments to Culver's bill, arrives; he has just held a press conference and has to go to another meeting, so he talks briefly about his amendments, and Culver promises to take care of them and thanks him for dropping by. Wallop mentions a concern that he has about a section of Culver's bill which would permit the government to make spot inspections of places that manufacture or distribute piperidine (two chemical companies and about twenty supply houses do so); he is worried about the appropriateness of such warrantless inspections, and he compares them with inspections under the Occupational Safety and Health Act, which is very unpopular among businesses, and whose warrantless-inspection provision has been held unconstitutional. Wallop is an easygoing man, and the discussion among the senators is low-key—just three men having a polite and respectful exchange. Culver explains that there is a difference between OSHA, which is designed to enforce civil compliance, and this bill, which is designed to prevent criminal activity, and that the question of what constitutes a minimum-notice requirement is going to be litigated soon. He talks quietly and reasonably; he likes Wallop, and treats his questions as responsible ones. Wallop suggests giving the companies one day's notice. Culver replies, "If they are cheating on the records, that would be all they would need." He adds, "I respect your sensitivity to this issue, because nothing is more threatening than the excessive encroachment of the state—invasions of privacy, and so on." He suggests that the subcommittee approve the bill as it is, that Wallop prepare an amendment, that the views of the Justice Department on this question be explored further, and that then he and Wallop discuss the issue on the Senate floor. Wallop agrees. Other questions raised by Wallop are similarly disposed of. It is all very civil and coöperative. One senses that Culver is doing this particular chore out of duty rather than out of passionate interest; he is doing it as carefully and responsibly as he can, but his heart does not seem to be in it.

When they move on to the bill covering the confiscation of the proceeds of illegal drug trafficking, Wallop asks, "How does somebody determine what the proceeds are?" After some discussion, which includes putting some questions to the committee staff, the senators agree that he has raised a good question, and that the language in the proposed bill needs to be made more specific. Culver suggests that Wallop's staff and the committee staff work together on the problem, puts off further consideration of that legislation, and, at ten-thirty-five, concludes the meeting. He has a briefing scheduled for ten-thirty, with Charles Stevenson, in preparation for the taping of a radio interview at eleven with Ike Pappas, of CBS, on the subject of the Navy. (He has turned down a CBS request for a television interview, on another subject, this week.)

On the way back to his office, Culver talks to me about the meeting we have just left. I ask him if he finds it frustrating that so much work has been put off until later. He replies, "No, that was useful. Some important questions got raised. That's what a markup is all about."

In his office, he talks again with Jim Larew about the weekend schedule for Iowa; Culver has some new thoughts. Then, in conversation with me, he returns to a subject that came up in the subcommittee meeting. One of the questions Wallop raised was whether there should be a "sunset" provision in the legislation they were considering—a provision that would automatically terminate the law unless Congress specifically reënacted it. "Sunset" provisions are viewed with increasing favor in Congress: the theory is that they force Congress to exercise its responsibility for oversight of the laws on the books, and that they can lead to the termination of outmoded programs. When Culver was in the House, he was one of the leaders of an effort to push Congress into taking its oversight responsibilities more seriously, but now he is worried that the "sunset" approach can be simplistic and can be overdone. "I'm all for sunset provisions," he says. "I think the oversight function is one of the most neglected things here. However, we have to give a great deal of thought to how to best accomplish this systematically. If you just take every piece of legislation and suggest a sunset provision, it can lead to problems. You can't have the governmental deck of cards falling down in an ad-hoc, episodic way. All of a sudden, we apprehend a dope peddler and he's home free. 'Oops, we forgot—that law lapsed last week.' With some things, the idea has particular appeal—for example, tax breaks—but even here you have to take a lot of things into account, including the need for a certain predictability."

Now Culver meets with Charles Stevenson. As he studies a memorandum Stevenson has given him on the Navy, he concentrates very hard, occasionally making notes on a yellow pad. One would think he was preparing for a final exam. Essentially, he knows the numbers and the status of the fleet, but he isn't taking chances. There is silence except for Culver's occasional questions to Stevenson or comments to the two of us. (The astute aides know when to be quiet.) Culver remarks, "The biggest shell game in town is with ship numbers. When the Navy wants to stress quantity, they count just about everything the Russians have that floats. But if they are really pressed, they acknowledge that we still have a margin of superiority, because of our higher quality. They keep changing their theme, and blur distinctions based on history, geography, and missions." Looking up from the notes at another point, he says, "So the real threat to the U.S. Navy is internal bad management—bad management, internal fights, the Rickover factor." He asks Stevenson if there are any other matters he wants to bring up. Stevenson tells him that Muskie, as chairman of the Intergovernmental Relations Subcommittee of the Governmental Affairs Committee, has held hearings on the Administration's proposals to reorganize the agencies that deal with civil defense, and that Muskie would like Culver's views on it. Culver is skeptical that the reorganization will lead to a resolution of questions of strategy and policy. He suggests that Stevenson read a transcript of the hearings over the weekend and give him a memorandum on them.

After the interview with Pappas, I ask Culver to talk to me a bit about the Carter Administration, and about his views, in general, on what constitutes effective political leadership. In a speech in March in Creston, Iowa, when not many Democrats were doing so, he defended Carter, as he did in his recent speech in Wisconsin. And, as I have heard him do more than once in his spontaneous conversation, he also defended the Great Society and the record of the Democratic Party. In Creston, he was in part attacking by implication Edmund G. Brown, Jr., the Governor of California, but he went on from there to say some other things; he departed from his prepared text and gave one of his red-faced, high-decibel performances. Speaking with passion, he told his audience, "Today, it is very fashionable and very trendy to say that less is better, that the Great Society, the New Frontier, failed." He continued, "Yes, we even have Democrats in our own party in high public places—who are interested in higher public places—who are going around now and saying, 'Mea culpa, we liberals have failed; you conservatives are right, the best government is no government.'" He said that such an attitude is dangerous, because only government can protect against fouled air, polluted water, phony drugs, consumer fraud, and monopolistic price-fixing. He said, "I am proud to have voted for historic legislation in the Great Society—for education, for health, conservation, civil rights. Those were exciting days. Those were the days when government had a commitment." Then he argued, as he often does, that the Great Society programs "weren't given a try." He talked about how much money went for the war in Vietnam. He said, "The federal government spent only about two billion dollars a year on the war on poverty—the same amount it spent every three weeks in the Vietnam War, blowing up rice paddies on the other side of the world." And, he said, when the Nixon Administration came along, "almost without exception, they put foxes in charge of the chicken coop in every single one of these departments." He continued, "Is it any wonder they didn't 'work'? Is it any wonder they 'failed'? When they were being administered by people who did not believe in them?"

Now, in our conversation, Culver talks about the Presidency. He says, "It seems to me that one of the interesting things is that there was a concern in the course of Carter's campaign for the nomination, and even in the general election, that he would be too 'political'—in the sense that he would not have a commitment to a philosophical course with any coherence and consistency. Some of that has to do with the nature of a primary campaign: you're called upon to get a percentage of the vote in a lot of different places, so you're really called upon to be cynical and dance around a lot of issues. So people were concerned about his fundamental motivations and his substantive sense. On balance, on the bigger issues I've found myself *relatively* comfortable—on the Cabinet choices, the Vice Presidential selection, and *some* important policy positions. The interesting thing, however, is that the Administration's greatest failure thus far has been in the process of figuring out how you get there from here. That has been a weaker part of the Administration than the instinct. I think the major role of a President is to set the agenda—priorities, or whatever you want to call it—and then set out to mobilize the essential elements of a constituency that is congenial in a basic way, that is sustainable and will give you a chance of achieving the larger goals. That approach presupposes that in choosing your issues and in choosing your fights and determining your compromises you are acting in the context of holding together those larger elements of your constituency. There are trade-offs to be made. You have to decide what you want to make a matter of principle, what you want to do with it. You have to decide where you want to compromise, where you're willing to alienate some part of the constituency—keeping in mind that you need at least fifty per cent to get there, and if you dissipate so much of the basic core of support in the quest for exquisite rationality, or, on the contrary, try to make everybody happy, to get ninety per cent by some kind of ad-hoc appeal on an issue, then you run the risk of total disarray. You fragment your base to the point where there is no base.

"So a President's problems could come somewhat from the bad habits of a Presidential-primary campaign: of yielding to the temptation to avoid taking firm positions; of worrying about the need to win a certain percentage here and a certain percentage there. It doesn't have to all add up; it can be apples and oranges. In the Presidency, you have to realize you're going to make some people happy and some people mad, and you have to decide how that's going to be sliced. After all, politics is the resolution of conflicting and competing interests and values and goals in a complex society, and it seems to me you have to be prepared to make, and even enjoy making, such decisions. You have to decide, for example, in the case of a marginal issue whether it's worth losing a United States senator, an important voice, or a major part of your constituency, or whether it's better to compromise. If the alternative is the replacing of that senator or that constituency group by someone who in the most fundamental way is opposed to your objectives, what have you gained? We all want to know what the merits are, and you want someone who will push public policy guided by that compass. But in the real cockpit of resolving these things you have to never lose sight of the need to compromise, and to know how to do it well, or even how to successfully effect a raw, naked deal. I'm not talking about something unethical, but you can give your support or withhold your support in order to reach some important goal. I like to believe I'm a purist, but you have to think through whether the position on a particular issue is worth the cost. I'm not saying it's easy, but maybe there are ways to keep from making everyone walk the plank too often. The cost-benefit factor has to be carefully calibrated. Presidential politics really consists of trying to determine what you want to do and then determine who in this country is inclined to support that. I realize that it sounds easy to say and that it's a lot harder to play that role creatively. But you can't reach a point where everybody has his nose out of joint—I mean everybody."

Culver continues, "That's what elections are about in this society: What course do you want to take and how do you build a coalition to reach those objectives? I'm really talking about how to do what you want to do: how to deal with Congress—when to fight and when not to fight, when to give and when not to give. And the same thing is true with the interest groups. But I think when you try to take each problem separately, like this"—Culver takes some pieces of paper and slaps them on his desk in different places—"there's no larger mosaic of what you want to achieve, no sense of the balances in reaching the larger purposes. In politics, it isn't bad to be political. It's so trendy now to think that politics is evil. But an astute and enlightened exercise of political power is what enables a democratic society to achieve its best potential. I don't know any other way to do it, except with the Plato kings."

Culver switches the subject slightly. He says, "When a constituent group comes in to see me and advocates a position and says, 'You represent all of us'—and, as it happens, my opponent took that view and I expressed my own views vigorously—I'll listen, but I'll make the point that I took my position in the campaign and the other guy lost. The lines have been drawn and the votes have been counted; if it makes a lot of people unhappy in the process, so be it. They were probably unhappy the day you won the election. That doesn't mean you're vindictive or unfair. But you've got a mandate to govern. One thing I find distasteful is where a member of Congress enjoys high voter approval—has a lot of credit in the bank—and yet still nervously puts his finger to the wind on each vote and is afraid to risk the slightest diminution of support by exerting leadership, even when he knows better. It should not be surprising that most people in politics, as elsewhere, would normally like to keep their jobs and have people approve of their work. But obviously in public service there are additional requirements. What is really disturbing and frustrating to me is when officeholders make it the be-all and end-all to stay in office, to the point where they cynically—and also as an ego trip—set out to broaden their base by making appeals to every conceivable group, and thereby weaken their commitment to a core set of principles or beliefs. They start to trim and cut. All of us can work for only so much in a passionate way, and you should work at those things with commitment and intensity. When you start running all around trying to appeal to a new constituency—to superficially throw a bone at a potential new vote—I think that's when you start finding yourself without any compass or purpose."

It's now twelve-forty-five, and Kennedy arrives to have lunch in Culver's office. Culver greets another visitor to his office, and gets around to saying goodbye to Phil Hilder, the staff member whom he did not have time to see yesterday. (It has occurred to Culver that Hilder might enjoy meeting Kennedy.) Kennedy makes a joke to me about Culver, and Culver wheels around and, trying to look very serious, says, "I was hoping I could have lunch with you, Ted, but I'm busy."

Kennedy laughs, and says to Culver, "You still stiff from the game?"

Culver answers, "I was never stiff."

Kennedy laughs again.

Culver and Kennedy have lunch together on occasion, sometimes with other friends, sometimes to talk about the Kennedy Institute of Politics. Today, they tell stories about Culver's postgraduate year in England, during which Kennedy went to visit him. Kennedy urges Culver to tell the stories and though he has undoubtedly heard them many times, breaks into great gales of laughter at Culver's telling of them once more. They also talk seriously, about such matters as current United States-Soviet relations, and about what is coming up in the Senate this afternoon, and what each is working on.

At two o'clock, Culver meets with five representatives of the Caterpillar Tractor Company and Deere & Company, manufacturers of earth-moving and farm equipment with plants in Iowa. Deere, with plants in five Iowa cities, is the largest employer in the state; and both companies are organized by the United Auto Workers, which has supported Culver (but was opposed to his position on the B-1 bomber). These companies export products, and the group that is here this afternoon wants to talk to Culver about the question of whether the National Environmental Policy Act should apply to international transactions. A representative of Caterpillar tells Culver that his firm is expanding in the Davenport area and may open a plant in Cedar Rapids, where Culver grew up. He says, "We represent a substantial constituency. We like the state of Iowa, and we could represent a larger constituency." He talks very smoothly, and he is not very subtle; Culver looks at him carefully and says nothing. The man continues, "This issue strikes us, Senator, as if it were a case of a bank in Cedar Rapids or Davenport being discriminated against, so, Senator, if you please . . ." The man goes on in this vein.

Culver tells the group that he will have to go to the Senate to vote at two-fifteen, and suggests that if they have not had enough time with him by then, they leave him some materials and discuss the problem further with a member of his staff.

Another man tells Culver that this group supports the Stevenson proposal to exempt the Export-Import Bank from coverage under the National Environmental Policy Act. He continues, "What we want to do is obtain your view on what kinds of issues we should consider."

Culver asks, "Did you cover our hearing the other day?"

The man says that he did.

"What did they tell you?" Culver asks. He asks it politely.

Another man tells him that they are concerned about the Administration policy that might emerge.

Then Culver asks them, "What if processes can be designed that might work? To what extent do you think there might be a positive sales advantage in selling products that were known to be environmentally safe? Maybe you could develop an international reputation in that regard. To what extent do you see an advantage in that approach?"

One of the men replies, "Very little. It would be seen cynically. People would say, 'America would stamp anything as sound.' "

Culver does not give up on trying to get them to think a bit differently, or, at least, get the drift of his thinking. He suggests that if "in terms of the kind of equipment you're selling, it was marked on the crate that it had been inspected for environmental safety, that might help."

One of the men says again that they would be concerned about the delay such a clearance might cause.

Culver says, "Do you think that we have any moral obligation—that if we find any commodity unfit for human consumption or a risk to safety and health we ought to be selling that stuff overseas?"

The buzzers signal a roll-call vote. Culver says, "Let's not worry before we have to worry. Let's see what the President comes up with, and see if we can live with it. Let's not prejudge it. Let's see if it puts you in a discriminatory position versus your international competition, and let's talk again. I think your point's well taken that we have not recognized the implications of the environmental policy for international policy and harmonized the two. I think it's clear that the congressional intent was that the act apply internationally, but that that hasn't been implemented. So the real question is, how is it going to apply? We're seeing the same thing in endangered species. I'm in the middle of that storm: How is it going to apply in reference to the competing interests? I think we should be competing vigorously internationally, and I think that if the rules are fair we can play." He praises the success of their industry, and talks about the importance of exports to the balance of payments. He asks them again to wait and see what policy the Administration comes up with. "I may or may not be able to agree with you on every point," he says, "but I want you to know how sincerely I solicit your views, and we'll stay in touch. Is that agreeable to you? O.K.?"

The group leaves, having had a hearing but having been promised nothing.

Culver goes to the floor to vote on an amendment to a bill to create a National Consumer Coöperative Bank. Just before lunch, Culver received a call from Ralph Nader asking him to oppose amendments that would weaken the bill. Culver had expressed some reservations about the bill, but, having talked with Mike Naylor and with some other senators in the course of the afternoon, has decided to support it. He returns to the office at three o'clock. Someone who had a two-forty-five appointment to see him has been waiting, and Jim Larew asks him if he has time to shake hands with someone else who has stopped by. He says that he does. There will be more votes, and Culver suggests to the person who has been waiting for the appointment that they go over to the Senate and he will talk with him in a nearby room between votes. "It's getting hectic," he says.

As the afternoon's votes proceed, Culver meets with a couple of visitors off the Senate floor and goes over with Dick Oshlo the letter he will send to Russell Long about beef imports. Afterward, Culver will have dinner with his two older daughters, Christina and Rebecca, who are in Washington, and with Leslie Dunlap, the librarian of the University of Iowa. Dunlap is working with him on a project in which Culver is intensely interested: a collection of more than two hundred letters that one of Culver's great-grandfathers, who grew up in Pennsylvania and enlisted as a volunteer in the Illinois infantry during the Civil War, wrote to his wife. Culver has worked on the project for ten years, and talks about it with excitement. A book of the letters is scheduled to be published under the auspices of the University of Iowa Library later this year. Culver is also having some letters translated that his maternal grandmother, who came from Sweden and settled in Minnesota, wrote to her family in Sweden. (Culver's heritage is a combination of English, Scotch, Irish, and Swedish.) Culver has shown me a picture of this grandmother and photostats of some of her letters. "I want to get this done for our kids, so they have something to build on," he said. Shortly before seven, he meets his daughters in his office.

Tomorrow, Culver is to leave for Iowa, and now it appears that the endangered-species bill may be brought up on Monday before he is scheduled to return. Members of his staff are trying to rearrange his schedule so that he can make his Monday-morning speech in Chicago at an earlier hour and get on an earlier flight to Washington, and Culver calls Robert Byrd to ask him to delay bringing up the bill until he has returned. Byrd's problem is that a number of senators will be out of town then, so he needs to have someone willing to bring up legislation on Monday. When he scheduled the endangered-species bill for Monday, he was unaware that Culver would not be back until that afternoon. When Culver talks to Byrd, he urges that the bill not be brought up before he returns on Monday. "I'm willing to coöperate on having it come up Monday," he tells Byrd. "Bob, it's really a major issue. I don't want to have something I've worked on this long come up before I'm here and when I'm not going to have control over it. Bob, I've held the hearings, I've done the markup. What I'd like is for you just to put something else on the schedule before three o'clock." Culver explains to me afterward that he understands that Byrd does have his problems. "There is always someone out of the country, someone out of town, someone who's sick, someone whose mother-in-law has died. There's considerable unpredictability in what we'll take up—much more of it here than in the House, where they try to set a predictable schedule. Here they make an effort to accommodate people—it's a luxury you can relatively afford, because of the smaller number." He urges Larew to try harder to get him back to Washington early on Monday, and goes off to dinner with Dunlap and his daughters.

6

FRIDAY, JULY 14TH: On the plane on the way to Iowa, Culver intently studies memorandums that his staff has prepared for him concerning the various appearances he will make today and tomorrow. We will spend Sunday at the Culvers' home in McGregor, and then return to Washington via Chicago. For each appearance, there is a separate blue folder containing materials on the meeting itself—where it is and at what time, who will be there, what the purpose is—and on the background of the issue that will be discussed (a copy of a bill and of a committee report are sometimes included), along with suggested "talking points" for Culver to use. Sometimes the memorandums tell Culver a good deal more than he needs to know. (One suggests that he "thank everyone for taking time to join you.")

Often, he is familiar with the issue, but it is his nature to study anyway—to bone up on the facts and figures and organize his thoughts, just as he does before he makes a Senate speech. Culver tells me on the plane, "With every meeting, you try to have as complete information as you can; so you're constantly working to be ready to tell people the status of things, the relevance to them. You're keeping up with a lot of stuff." Now Culver is boning up on the subjects of noise control, railroad crossings, tuition tax credits, soil conservation (he has won Senate authorization for funds for a program to deal with the effects of soil erosion on water pollution, thus going at two problems at once, and is now trying to get the money appropriated), beef imports, and more. Before he left Washington this morning—at shortly after eleven o'clock—he went over the schedule for the trip again with Jim Larew; signed mail; arranged with Dick Oshlo to have material for the endangered-species debate that is to begin on Monday telecopied to his Des Moines office. This morning, Culver was told that Gaylord Nelson had been lobbying Gary Hart, who had supported Culver's endangered-species compromise, to oppose it. Before he left Washington, Culver tried to reach Hart, but he was unable to.

On the plane, Culver is sitting, as he requested, in an aisle seat, but still, this huge man seems scrunched in a small space. From time to time during our ride, Culver breaks off from his studying to tell me something about Iowa, ask about something in the newspapers I'm reading, or volunteer a thought about politics, but mainly he concentrates on his folders. At one point, he says, "You know, groups are always in your office wanting something more. They never say, 'We've tried such-and-such a program, and it doesn't work. So thank you very much; we don't want it anymore.' Meanwhile, states cut back on what they're doing, so people turn to the federal government. There are all these states that have surpluses. That they're in the shape they're in is why we're in the shape we're in."

At O'Hare Airport, in Chicago, where we are to change planes, Culver checks with his office and then, over coffee, talks about the Senate. "The hard thing is to stay with something—to cope with the fatigue of fighting for something and the psychological pressure not to do so. You're working with peers, and it's easier to have everything be pleasant. The difficult thing is to do something constructive and retain your relationships; it's another version of Sam Rayburn's 'If you want to get along, go along'—a more sophisticated version. You could sit back and enjoy it and accept the perks and the psychic gratification, such as it is, but then no public purpose is served. And there *is* a little need for the 'You scratch my back, I'll scratch yours.' So you have to develop a reputation for integrity in your opposition and for being fair and keeping your word—but within that context you have to be willing to take on some uncomfortable things and still go to work every day. The whole thing is cutting edge: you can't worry too much about being loved; at some time, you have to decide, 'Let's go! Bang!' If the others know that it's not a cheap shot, that often you might be right, they'll still respect you."

When a member of the House is elected to the Senate, as Culver was in 1974, he makes a big leap in the number of constituents he must deal with, the amount of territory he must cover. Iowa, for example, has six congressional districts. Moreover, it is a state with many towns and several relatively large ones, each served by its own local media—the "media market"—and therefore is not that simple for a politician to cover. It has a larger proportion of cropland than any other state and over ninety per cent of the state's area is used for farming of one sort or another, yet slightly more of its people work in industry than on farms—though much of the industry is oriented toward agriculture. The population is largely of German and Scandinavian descent, with some Irish (especially in Dubuque), and the black population is slightly more than one per cent. It is a proud state: its slogan is "A place to grow." It has the highest literacy rate in the nation. Its pamphlets boast of its native-born: Buffalo Bill and Henry Wallace and Herbert Hoover and Glenn Miller and Johnny Carson. It is in the center of the United States in several respects: it is twenty-fifth in population, and twenty-fifth in area. Its geographical position—which also places it in just about the center of the country—sets it somewhat apart from other Midwestern states, and from the Plains States, to its west; Minnesota is to its north, and Missouri is to its south. The fact that the state, which had traditionally been a Republican one, has in recent years produced three Democratic senators (Harold Hughes, who was first elected governor in 1962 and then senator in 1968; Dick Clark, elected in 1972; and Culver) is attributable to a number of things: industrialization and the movement of the population to the cities; a populist streak embodied in the old progressive and agrarian radical movements; and the Democrats' development of modern, computerized precinct-by-precinct methods of organizing. The state has four Democrats and two Republicans in the House of Representatives, a Republican governor, and a Democratic legislature; it backed Ford for the Presidency in 1976.

Our plane is late, and arrives in Des Moines at two-thirty-five—five minutes after Culver was to be at his first event. A local staff member meets us to drive us to the meeting, and in the car on the way Culver goes over a press release, telecopied from Washington, that is to be issued here; he finds a mistake in one figure. He reads the draft of a letter—also sent out—that Edmund Muskie has suggested that Culver and he send to Adlai Stevenson about Stevenson's proposal to exempt the Export-Import Bank from the requirement of the National Environmental Policy Act that certain federal agencies must prepare a statement on the environmental impact of their activities. Culver decides that he has some questions about the letter, and tells his staff man to tell his Washington office that he is not ready to sign it and will try to discuss it later. "I have to focus on other things now," he says. And, his impatience beginning to show through, he says to the staff man, "Let's go. Let's go." (It has been said that it is not one of the more pleasant jobs to be a driver for him in a campaign.)

The first meeting, at the Des Moines City Hall, is with city and state officials who are interested in noise control. In March, Culver's Resource Protection Subcommittee held a field hearing in Des Moines on the subject. Now he sits at the end of a long table in a conference room. Three microphones are in front of him—two from radio stations and one from a television station. (Don Brownlee has sent a schedule to the Des Moines news media.) "I thought I'd bring you up to date on what's going on in Washington in the area of noise control," Culver tells the group. "Maybe I'll just start out by announcing that the State of Iowa and the City of Des Moines have been awarded a series of grants." He then says that Des Moines has been awarded fifteen thousand dollars for research on noise control, and the state twenty thousand dollars. His announcement, and his being here, will force him into the news. He goes on to say that a bill, the Quiet Communities Act of 1978, to extend the authorization of the Noise Control Act of 1972 has been approved by his subcommittee and by the full Environment and Public Works Committee, and will be brought to the Senate floor soon. He tells the group that as a result of the subcommittee's oversight hearings the decision was made that the priorities and the emphasis of the existing noise-control program should change—from a concern with the noise level of various kinds of machinery to an effort to help communities work out ordinances to deal with noise problems. Having studied the committee report on the plane, he now tells the group the details of the new bill. "After all those years and millions of dollars, all they could tell us was that bulldozers are noisy," Culver says. "And it doesn't matter if you get the noise of products down if you don't get local ordinances."

Elaine Szymoniak, a Des Moines city councilwoman and an audiologist, who testified before Culver's hearing in March, says, "We certainly want to thank you. We were very grateful for the opportunity to express our views." She continues, "I never thought I might be sitting in a situation like this. It's really exciting to see some things develop."

Culver tells her that her testimony was very persuasive and had an impact on the bill. He talks to the group a while longer, asking members a number of specific questions about noise problems in Des Moines, suggesting that they send him information on certain matters, offering to send them copies of the new bill and the committee report.

Culver gives a brief television interview about his noise-control announcement to a reporter from WHO-TV, in Des Moines, and then gets back into the car to go to the next stop. In the car, he ascertains from the staff member driving him that the incorrect figure in the press release—it said that he was announcing an award of thirty-five thousand dollars to Des Moines for noise control, rather than fifteen thousand dollars—was not corrected, and he jokes, with uncharacteristic resignation, "Well, I'll just have to get them more money."

At the next stop, an unsafe railroad crossing just outside Des Moines (the site was chosen to provide a "visual" for television), Culver stands with two county engineers and announces that he has been able to get the Environment and Public Works Committee to approve a change in the Federal-Aid Highway Act which will permit Iowa to get more funds to make crossings safer. This particular crossing has a faded "Railroad Crossing" sign and a stop sign, but no lights, and it is at a bad angle to the road, so that a driver might not see an oncoming train. He says that under the existing law the funds were allocated on the basis of a state's population and area and the number of its miles of United States mail routes, rather than on the number of its railroad crossings. Citing figures from memory, he explains that this meant that Puerto Rico and Alaska received far more money per railroad crossing than Iowa did. A camera crew from KCCI-TV, also in Des Moines, is here, and it films Culver as he stands at the crossing making his announcement and asking one of the engineers some questions, and then as the TV reporter interviews him. He is setting the agenda: he has been as deliberate in this as he is in just about everything else. In the hour and a half that he has been in Iowa, he has got on the two major Des Moines television stations, making announcements on matters of interest here and showing that, back in Washington, he is working for Iowa. He has not, by contrast, put himself in situations where he is answering questions about Andrew Young or the Soviet trials of dissidents or labor-law reform. He has stayed on the offensive. When a politician returns to his state, it is useful if people know he is there, and the best way to make sure that they know he is there is to get on television.

Next, we drive to Ames, about forty minutes away, for a meeting with the dean of the College of Agriculture of Iowa State University and other university and state officials. Along the way, there is evidence that this is a good crop year: there has been plenty of rain, and the corn is about five feet high and the tassels are out—very good for mid-July. The subject in Ames is to be something called a Soil Tilth Center, which the university wants to establish, and for which Culver and Clark have written to the Agriculture Subcommittee of the Senate Appropriations Committee seeking an appropriation of one hundred thousand dollars. On the plane ride out here, when I saw Culver reading a brochure on the subject, I asked him, apologetically, what tilth was. Not pretending that he was terribly sure himself, he said that it had to do with the composition of the soil, and that we would have an opportunity to talk about it with the people at Ames, which is renowned around the world for its agricultural expertise. At Ames, Culver is seated in a classroom, along with six state and university people. The dean sits in the teacher's chair and talks to him about soil erosion. It's hot in the classroom, and Culver takes off his jacket and rolls up his sleeves. A reporter from the university newspaper is here. Culver asks the group some questions and talks with them in an informed way about soil erosion, a serious problem in some parts of Iowa.

One of the men says that deterioration of the land is taking place at an alarming rate. "Without tilth research," he says, "we're going to have to abandon some of these areas."

Culver mentions the letter that he and Clark have written to the subcommittee. Then the men take us out to some research fields to show us the differences between plots of land that have been given different kinds of treatment. Culver asks them if they would explain to me what, exactly, tilth is.

The dean says, smiling, "It's very difficult to define; it's usually thought of as good condition of the soil," and he asks one of the others if he will "take a crack" at explaining it to us. The other scratches his head, and relays the question to a third.

This man describes tilth as "organic matter, consistency of the soil, the structure of the soil," and finally another of the men laughs and says,

"You see, Senator, that's why we need the lab—to find out what it is."

At six-thirty, Culver reaches his office in the Federal Building in Des Moines. He sits at a desk with flags on either side of it, in a sort of replica of a Senate office, and talks with representatives of the Iowa State Education Association and the Iowa Association of School Boards about tax credits for tuition payments to private elementary and secondary schools. These groups are opposed to the tax credits. It is an hour earlier in Iowa than it is in Washington; it has been a long day, and Culver is weary now. He agrees with their position on tax credits—he tells them that straightaway—and he is already familiar with the arguments that they are making, but they have come (some of them from distant cities) to talk to their senator, so he forces himself to focus and listen. The meeting breaks up at seven o'clock. Culver receives a message that has been relayed from his Washington office that Robert Byrd has agreed not to bring up the endangered-species bill before four o'clock on Monday. Culver still wants to try to get back to Washington early, to prepare for the debate. He goes over a press release that is to be issued about a meeting he will hold with some cattlemen tomorrow, and, after a quick cleanup and change, goes to a dinner at the Des Moines Club.

The host of the dinner is John Chrystal, a banker and farmer and former state banking official (under Hughes), who is also the nephew of the late Roswell Garst, whose farm Nikita Khrushchev visited in 1959. The Garst farm is to Iowa something like what the King Ranch is to Texas. The Des Moines Club is at the top of one of the new buildings in the city's downtown area; about a dozen people are here, most of them strong supporters of Culver. Chrystal tells me that he is proud of all three Democrats whom Iowa has sent to the Senate in recent years and that what he appreciates most about Culver are his passion about issues and his intellect. Moreover, Chrystal says, "he'll tell me to go to hell." Culver asks the people at the dinner what they think about "the whole U.S.-Soviet thing," and one of them replies, "I think we're both acting crazy." The guests ask Culver a number of questions, and, as he replies, he starts talking—as he does when he gets very involved—in a stream. He talks about arms sales—about how years ago he began to urge that the United States talk with the Soviet Union about the possibility of reaching agreement on the reduction of arms sales around the world, and how such talks have now begun. (In 1975, Culver sent a letter to Henry Kissinger saying that the conventional-arms-sales race was "madness" and urging that there be an international conference of major arms producers, and subsequently a hundred and two members of the House and the Senate signed another letter to this effect, sponsored by Culver. Kissinger responded that there would be no conference but that he would work on the matter through "quiet diplomacy." Later that same year, Culver and Walter Mondale, then a senator, won enactment of an amendment calling for such a conference. During the 1976 campaign, Jimmy Carter picked up the idea for the conference, and last December a conference between the United States and the Soviet Union began in Helsinki.)

Culver, discussing arms sales, says, "Isn't it insane?" He talks about the need for converting industries dependent upon arms sales to other activities. (It is extremely rare to hear a politician talk about such a thing.) He tells them about the Armed Services Committee—about how the Republicans on the committee offered an amendment to add six billion dollars to the committee's defense-budget recommendations, and how he countered by suggesting that they amend that to say that taxes had to be raised the same amount. He tells them that when he asked in a committee meeting whether the amount approved by the committee exceeded the Administration's request, Strom Thurmond suggested that if it did they should take the money from the funds for food stamps, and that he replied, "Yeah, the people who get that aren't around here knocking on the door." He talks about the fact that the United States has nine thousand warheads to the Soviet Union's forty-two hundred warheads, and he explains in some detail the technical difficulties that the Soviet Union would have in knocking out our land-based missiles—a subject at issue in the debate over SALT. He discusses the fairly widespread assumption that the Soviet Union is not as technologically advanced as the United States is. He says, "The Soviet general who comes in and says, 'Let's fire our missiles,' you know, he probably couldn't get his bathtub to work that morning"—at this, Culver moves his hands as if struggling with faucets—"or get the elevator up to the war room." He talks about "the people in the think tanks who draw up these bloodless schemes," and, as he had to me in Washington, about how both countries can be seen as preparing for civil defense, and about the differences in the histories and geographies of the United States and the Soviet Union. He is asked about the Carter Cabinet. He says that he is largely pleased with it, but he points out that he was one of five Democrats who voted against the confirmation of Griffin Bell as Attorney General. "I finished reading 'Why Not the Best?' and got Griffin Bell," he says. He is asked about the Middle East, about the sale of AWACS to Iran, and about inflation; he answers the questions thoughtfully. He is teaching these people as well as responding to them.

Around ten-thirty, we leave the dinner to fly on a small chartered plane to Moline, Illinois, one of the "Quad Cities," on the border of Illinois and Iowa. Tomorrow morning, Culver must be in Davenport for the meeting with the cattlemen.

7

SATURDAY, JULY 15TH: At breakfast, Culver talks with Patsy Grace, who runs his Davenport office, and George Gilbert, one of his Washington aides, who works on agricultural matters. Last night, after arriving at his motel, he was briefed by Gilbert for the meeting with the cattlemen. This morning, Culver tells me that he is sympathetic toward the beef producers but that he also tries to be careful about doing things that could encourage foreign retaliation harmful to over-all United States trade interests. He explains the cattlemen's problem: that they had four bad years, and then, when prices finally went up, Carter announced that he would permit the importation of more beef into the United States. The amount by which Carter increased the imports, he continues, was not enough to lower meat prices for consumers by an appreciable amount but was enough to upset the cattlemen. (Yesterday, in Topeka, Kansas, Vice President Mondale announced that the President was not considering price controls for meat, and that he rejected "open-ended meat imports." The story is on the front page of today's Des Moines *Register*.) The problem, Culver explains, is that the action has shaken the cattlemen's confidence, so that they might cut down on the number of cattle they raise for next year, thus forcing prices up again.

On the way to the meeting with the cattlemen, Culver goes over (again) the press release that is to be issued, and the briefing material that Gilbert has prepared for him—about beef prices, about speculation in the cattle market, about nutrition, about livestock brokers, about legislation pending in Congress. Most of the cattle producers in Iowa are small businessmen, entrepreneurs, and are considered essentially Republican, but they are important to the state beyond their numbers, because other parts of its economy depend on them, and it is not out of the question that they would support a Democrat. Unlike other agricultural groups—grain producers, for example—they tend not to ask for government help. In the car, Culver asks Patsy Grace if she knows whether the meeting will be covered by television. She says she thinks that it will. He studies the briefing material with the same intensity and concentration that he devoted to the material for a CBS interview last week and that he gives to preparing for a speech.

At nine o'clock, Culver meets at Ray Doyle's farm with nine men who are present and past officials of the state and county cattlemen's associations and with other cattlemen from the area. It is a warm day. Culver—tieless, and with his shirtsleeves rolled up—leans against the fence of a cattle pen and talks with the men.

One of them tells him, "I would like to say one thing, Senator, and that is that we as farmers have no way of setting our price, and we get penalized when it gets profitable."

Culver turns to one of the men, Waldo Mommsen, a past president of the Iowa Cattlemen's Association, and says, "What do you think, Waldo, about getting farmers to petition the exchange market and getting some of that swing cut down?" (His press release is about the swings in prices, suggesting that cattle prices have fallen by more than the increase in imports warranted, and saying, "I think Iowa cattlemen are on the right track in suspecting futures trading on the Chicago Exchange as being the source of much of this instability.")

Mommsen says, "Yes, there's too much of a swing."

Another man says, "Anyone feeding cattle knows the gamble. When we take our lumps, the Administration doesn't help us, and we didn't ask for help, but when we're not taking our lumps we don't like the Administration coming in and taking it away."

Another asks, "Why do they pick on beef? They say the price is too high. Compared to what?"

Culver says, "They never gave you an award for fighting inflation in the four years you were losing money."

WQAD television turns up, and also a newspaper reporter carrying a camera.

Culver tells the group about the resolution he has introduced criticizing the President's action.

One of the men says, "Yeah, I've seen that. It's very good."

Culver tells them the purpose of his resolution is to "help restore confidence," and another of the men says, "You got a long way to go."

Another asks, "Why did they do it?"

Culver replies, "Inflation. Someone figured 'Don't just stand there, do something,' and they didn't understand what it would do psychologically. And they don't look ahead to what it would do to long-term supplies, how it would get people to thin out their supplies and therefore lead to more shortage."

Culver reasons with them, shows them that he

understands their problem and is trying to help them, and at the same time avoids saying things that will inflame them or raise their expectations unrealistically.

One of the men, referring to the fact that Administrations usually take actions to please farmers in Presidential-election years, says to Culver, "I think it's good for you to come out. There's problems out here, except when we have an election."

From Davenport, we fly on another small plane to Cedar Rapids, the state's second-largest city, where Culver grew up.

On the plane, I ask Culver how he can be such a defender of liberal programs and the Great Society in an essentially white state.

He replies, "I think there's a fairness in Iowa. I don't think it's easily stampeded. They reject demagoguery. Joe McCarthy never got much of a foothold in Iowa. There's a compassionate side, and there's even an internationalist side, through the state's interest in world trade—and not just in agricultural products. Cedar Rapids has the highest per-capita export business of any landlocked city in America—farm equipment, road-building equipment. And Quaker Oats is there, too. All this gives the state a sophistication, and vital strains that, properly appealed to, will support very progressive purposes."

I ask Culver to talk to me about the subject of "single-issue politics" which he spoke of in his speech in Wisconsin in June. His speech pointed to the increasing difficulty politicians have in performing their function as mediators, as the ones who work out compromises among the competing interests in this country. I ask him why he thinks this problem developed.

Culver replies, "There is a new political creed of cynicism, of selfishness, of personal concerns instead of public causes. I think that we're at the conjunction of two cycles in our national life. One was probably predictable, the other is exceptional. I think that now, in the seventies, we are in a somewhat historically familiar repose after a period of exertion, just as in the twenties there was a 'return to normalcy.' I think that we do have periods where there is a very aggressive expansion of rights or a very strong national effort of some kind or other, and then there is a period of reconciliation of those newfound rights—arguably, this endangered-species issue is an example of that. So, to the extent that we're in such a period, it's a quite natural phenomenon. I think that the second thing is more exceptional—the discontent, the meanness, the sourness of the national electorate. I think that's attributable primarily to the disenchantment with the national leadership over Vietnam and Watergate. And added to that are the recent peccadillos of Congress—'Koreagate'—and even the increased complexity of our problems, such as our economic situation, where we used to have either recession or inflation. The one virtue that those problems had was that they were incompatible, and now we're finding that even that is not true. I think that with this breakdown of trust and confidence you see a readiness on the part of the electorate to substitute instantaneously its judgment for that of the elected official. That trust is a very delicate thing, and once it's destroyed it takes a long time to restore it."

He continues, "We see that breakdown not only between the electorate and the Congress but we also see it internally in the Congress between the membership and their leadership, and we see it between the Congress and the executive branch. So you don't have the cohesion, the cement that is usually present in these relationships. Further, the problems are of such enormous complexity that the public is frustrated and senses it can't influence these situations by traditional forms of political action, and so it turns in other directions. People are increasingly turning to issues that they feel they can understand and do feel strongly about, and are devoting all their energy and resources to one particular issue. For a lot of reasons, the parties have lost their strength, their traditional power as the reconcilers of competing interests. So you've had balkanization into these splinter groups. When you have these rifle-shot constituencies, with their money and discipline, their influence on the outcome of elections is obviously disproportionate to their numbers. You can form a necklace of all these single-issue constituencies devoid of common purpose or values, and an unprincipled politician can cynically exploit them."

I ask Culver if he thinks this is a temporary phenomenon.

He replies, "There's one theory that sees the current malaise as temporary, but what worries me is that there are profoundly disturbing signs that this mood of disillusionment and cynicism is altering the practical realities of political representation and distorting the value of public service." He continues, "The danger is that we're getting to the point where the lack of trust threatens the very basis of our system of government, which is, after all, based on the consent of the governed. Traditionally, we have had an acceptance of the notion that we are a republic, where an elected official is given a franchise for a certain period of time—two, four, six years—to represent as best he can the interests of his constituents as well as contribute his own best judgment. He has a dual responsibility: to constituency and conscience, and sometimes they're compatible and sometimes they're not. Presumably, the franchise is an endorsement of our judgment. Edmund Burke said that a representative must not be 'ready to take up or lay down a great political system for the convenience of the hour . . . he is in Parliament to support his opinion of the public good, and does not form his opinion in order to get into Parliament, or to continue in it.' And now even that very basic notion of the way our form of democracy should function is under siege. Obviously, officials who consistently vote against the wishes of their constituents will not and should not be returned to office. But we should be expected to do more than simply mirror the momentary mood of the public. We hear so much today about people wanting strong leaders, but there's a certain contradiction in at the same time demanding leaders who do not lead but follow."

He continues, "I think also that now the whole situation is complicated by people's fear concerning their own economic circumstances. With inflation, the great American middle class, which has to be the engine that provides the national impulse, is, for quite understandable reasons, fearful. And, when the electorate is fearful, obviously it's not going to be particularly generous or concerned with the needs of others. In the sixties, when we had relative affluence, the climate was ripe for a very magnanimous commitment, and then that was overtaken by events we've been talking about. And so now we're in a situation where, rather than having a public acting on its best impulses, it's vulnerable to an exploitation of the more mean-spirited side of human nature."

So, I ask Culver, if one is a politician who cares about the things Culver cares about, what does one do?

"Leadership is being willing to set the agenda for the nation and stating what is the unfinished business," he says. "This will clearly require a positive role for government. Our problem is, we haven't stayed on a sustained or steady course—I think that you have to just try something and stay with it long enough to make it work. We have such an intolerance of any failure or shortcoming when it comes to dealing with the intractable social problems. There are too many fits and starts; we just don't have the staying power.

"I'm reading a new book by John Gardner called 'Morale,' and he talks about the importance of staying power: that just because everything can't be made perfect overnight we can't give up, that we have to keep working at it and you can't be disillusioned when the progress is painfully slow. It's always going to be imperfect; there are always going to be inequities; there are always going to be these problems. But you can't just do nothing or throw up your hands in despair; you can't just give something a try for a few minutes. It requires enormous acts of leadership and education to create the requisite public understanding—whether we're talking about foreign aid or some of our domestic problems that don't command natural constituencies. For eight years, we didn't have a government that had the soul and the will and the commitment to deal with these problems; it lacked any real public purpose. Obviously, you have to take a critical look at what seems to work and what doesn't, but you should give all programs rigorous scrutiny. It's only to be expected that some of our efforts to alleviate intractable problems won't be successful, and we must be willing to make adjustments. But when you find imperfections, that doesn't necessarily mean that you repudiate the whole commitment. I think you only have to talk sense to people, that you have to hit it head on, that you have to explain what's happening. And I still have sufficient confidence that if the public knows the facts it will respond. The kind of political leadership that I respect and admire has to have some genuine passion to it; it has to have some very real and heartfelt objectives and goals and desires in terms of a better and more just society."

Culver continues, "All of this gets back to that dual responsibility of an elected official: to represent and reflect the interests and attitudes of the electorate, and even their prejudice on occasion, and also to educate public opinion. However, people are increasingly saying, 'I didn't elect you to offer your judgment. I elected you to reflect and mirror anything I want, any time of day, any hour.' And of course once you accept that premise—and unfortunately there are too many public officials who will—then it's clear it doesn't matter who you elect to the job; it doesn't matter one bit, if we subscribe to that definition of what representative government is all about. One should have settled principles and convictions. Otherwise, you're on a slippery slope and there's no end to it. It has been my experience that if you just vote any way you think is right and you have your reasons and you can defend that vote, and defend it with conviction, the people will respect that. Similarly, in Congress you live by your reputation just as much as anywhere else. People turn to those they trust and those they respect, and if you're known as someone who has thought about a problem before you reached a decision you're not going to be subjected to all kinds of pressures and threats. They know you're not the kind of person who will respond to that. They don't think less of you for it; they think more of you. We all understand that people in Congress have to represent the interests of their districts or states and that Congress is a cockpit where you bang heads and try to reconcile all the competing interests. However, if people aren't willing to also lead and take risks, I don't really see why they are there. If they're there only to get reëlected, what's the purpose of it? If you aren't going to contribute your own judgment, anybody can do the job and there isn't any real issue as to which person could do it better, or is more qualified, or has higher personal character and integrity, or anything else."

Our plane has a flat tire when we land at the Cedar Rapids airport, and the pilot has some trouble steadying it. (As it skids off the runway onto some grass, a voice from the control tower says, "Please stay off the grass.") Once it is clear that we are utterly safe, and all is calm and we are waiting at the far end of the field for someone to come and get us, Culver jokes, "Can I do something courageous while we're waiting?" Then, as he gets out of the plane, he says, "I'll go douse the engines and be right back to save you."

Our first stop in Cedar Rapids will be at a lunch with officials of the Collins divisions of Rockwell International. Collins makes aviation and telecommunications equipment and is the second-largest employer in the state; about ten thousand people work for it, in Cedar Rapids. Collins and its parent company had a stake in the B-1 bomber, which Culver played a major role in killing. Rockwell was already doing research and development on the proposed new bomber and would have been the largest contractor for it, and Collins would have supplied some equipment. In the course of Rockwell's lobbying for the B-1, its officials were reported to have told some Senate offices that the amendment that Culver successfully pushed in 1976 to postpone funding for the bomber (thus giving a new Administration an opportunity to review the matter) would further the objectives of the Soviet Union. Glare Rice, now president of the Collins group and then vice president of one of its divisions, appeared on television and wrote an article in the Cedar Rapids *Gazette* opposing Culver's attempt to kill the plane, saying, "People who have opposed the B-1 have, frankly, distorted the facts."

He said they had surrounded the argument with a "cloud of fiction." Culver replied in the paper, countering Rice's arguments in detail and saying that the facts "suggest that the fiction rests with the uncritical opponents of prudent delay." Then he pointed out that "Rockwell International has an obvious financial interest in approval of the B-1 program," cited President Eisenhower's warning " 'against the acquisition of unwarranted influence . . . by the military-industrial complex,' " and said that the ultimate decisions on such defense programs must be made "by our civilian leadership and elected representatives."

Now Rice and William Strathern, another official of Collins, are at the Cedar Rapids airport to meet us. The Collins officials have been seeking this meeting for some time. Culver is in a position to be helpful to them, and, as it happens, he has his own interest in making peace with them. Last year, he put a statement in the *Congressional Record* commending the company for winning a major defense contract to provide a tactical navigation system for aircraft which improves readiness and reduces maintenance costs.

On the way to the Collins plant, Culver and the officials make pleasant conversation about Cedar Rapids. Strathern tells Culver how pleased they were with the item in the *Congressional Record.* Rice says that Collins, whose plant covers forty acres, is "the largest single employer in any one location in Iowa." (Deere & Company employs more people, but in scattered plants.)

After we arrive at the Collins headquarters, a company photographer takes pictures of Culver standing with the officials outside the building. He has on his tie and jacket now, and he looks somber.

Thirteen men, including the Washington representative of Rockwell, meet with Culver in the boardroom. Noting that it is Saturday afternoon,

Culver remarks, "I wonder how many votes I've lost interrupting golf games." The group laughs appreciatively. He goes on, "I assure you I'll be out of here soon. I do want you to know what genuine pride I do have in the Collins company. You can't grow up in this city and not have an appreciation of what Collins means to this city and this state and the country. It's a source of pride to me as a member of the Senate Armed Services Committee, working on arms-procurement bills, to hear the praise of Collins products on a day-to-day basis. And when I go to military installations in the United States and around the world, I inquire about the Collins products and I always hear the highest praise." He continues, getting to what is on the mind of everyone in the room, "So although, as you know, we differ on what should be built, I hope that, once the decisions are made about what should be built, as much of it as possible is by Collins." He adds, "Sometimes you don't get that perception from reading the newspapers."

Then we sit down at a long table, and while we eat a sandwich lunch Rice stands on a rostrum and presents a slide show about the Collins company. Culver interrupts to talk of his concern about the readiness of our aircraft and ships—he wants to demonstrate to each group he meets with that he is knowledgeable about what it is doing and is interested in its problems—and then, having got involved in the subject, and realizing that he is going on some, he says, "I don't want to take time here. I'm here to learn from you, and you can't learn much with your mouth open." When, after a while, Rice mentions a United Airlines order from Boeing, for which Collins will supply materials, Culver cites the figure that is the amount of the contract. He comes across as well informed, because he is well informed.

Culver asks some questions about the company's success in supplying products for NATO, and Rice says that there is a problem—that the French will buy only French equipment, that the Germans will buy only German equipment. The lack of "commonality" of NATO equipment is a problem that Culver has been concerned about. "We've really got a military museum over there rather than a combined force," he says. "It's incredible. They can't supply each other, they can't equip each other, they can't repair each other. You have twenty-three different kinds of aircraft and seven different kinds of tanks—even hoses and water nozzles." He says, "This is an area I've been particularly active in—pushing NATO commonality and inter-operability. If you have any ideas or thoughts, I'd like to hear them, and maybe if you can tell me who in your shop is following this we can send you some of our amendments and you can tell me what effects they might have." He is doing business on various levels here.

When the officials tell him that they want to make another slide presentation, he glances at his watch—we're running a little late now—but sits patiently through another slide show. Then the division heads who are present want to tell him about their activities, and about concerns they have in dealing with the Defense Department. They tell him about their current competition with Texas Instruments and Magnavox for a major new contract, and make an implicit plea for help. Says one of the officials, "You could say it's Iowa against Texas and California."

At the Linn County Juvenile Detention Center, in Marion, about a half hour's ride from Cedar Rapids, Culver is met by Josy Gittler, the chief counsel of his Juvenile Delinquency Subcommittee. Culver has been interested in the confinement of juveniles, particularly status offenders (people who have not actually committed a crime but are in trouble, such as runaways and truants): he wants to support efforts to keep them from being sent to prisons along with people who have committed serious crimes. Miss Gittler drafted a model juvenile code for the State of Iowa, and Culver made some phone calls to help get it through the state legislature earlier this year. This center is a "secured" (locked) facility for juveniles who have committed or have been charged with committing crimes and are awaiting trial or placement; Culver's briefing paper tells him that this is the best juvenile-detention center in the state. The center is a modern one-story building. Some newspaper reporters and two television crews are here. Culver suggests that they wait while he tours the facility, and says that he will visit with them afterward; he also asks them to take care not to photograph the detainees' faces, in order to protect their privacy.

After Culver has toured the facility, he talks with five young men who are currently being held here. They sit on chairs lined up in a row, and he sits facing them. He talks to them quietly. He tells them that he has been doing some work "for people like you, who have some problems or have got in trouble—about the facilities for you, and maybe some of the things that got you in here."

Miss Gittler has reminded him that he saw one of the boys, whom I shall call Francis, at another county facility, which he toured in the fall.

"Francis, I saw you before," Culver says now. "I thought you were doing pretty good. What happened?"

Francis tells him about a number of times that he "got in trouble."

Culver asks Francis if his parents know where he is.

He says that they do but that he hasn't heard from them.

"Do your sisters or brothers know where you are?" Culver asks.

"No," Francis says.

Culver asks if he's talked to a lawyer.

Francis tells him that one came to talk with him for five minutes.

Culver then talks to the group about seeing kids with burns on their arms "from playing around with cigarette butts"—a game that is a form of "chicken"—and he asks if any of them have been doing that.

One says that he has.

"I hope you're not doing that anymore," Culver says softly. "That's pretty dumb."

One wonders what they think of this large man sitting here, whether they understand who he is. He asks how many of them have been in jail before. Four raise their hands. He asks how many of them have parents who are divorced (three) and how many come from families with drinking problems (three).

Francis says, "Not mine. My dad spent it all on gambling and then he'd come home and beat my mom."

Culver asks how many of them were beaten severely at home. Two raise their hands.

He asks what the others are here for. Two tell him they are here for burglary; one says he has been involved in grand larceny.

Culver turns to one and says, gently, "What were you thinking about then—when you got involved in the burglary? What do you want to do with your life? Do you think that what you've been doing will lead to the kind of life you want to lead?"

The young man replies, "Some interesting people were doing it."

Culver says, "Why would you want to go along

with them? You look strong enough to be disciplined enough not to go along with them."

Culver talks with the boys a little longer, thanks them for talking with him, tells them he wishes them well with their lives, and shakes hands with each of them. "Francis," he says, "can't we work it so the next time we see each other it won't be in one of these places? Huh? Wouldn't you be happier? Huh? I'd be happier."

Then Culver is interviewed by the television reporters. One asks him about his activities in the state this weekend, and Culver once more sets the agenda. He talks about the detention center and his interest in the confinement of juveniles. "I think this facility is the best in the state," he says. "These people have actually committed a crime or are charged with a crime, and these are cases where they need a secure facility. This shows the possibility of having some more humane facility and of keeping them out of jail with hardened criminals." He goes on to talk about juvenile delinquency and about "the common themes" that one finds in so many of the cases, including the cases he has just heard about: "poverty, families that are dysfunctional—which really means that they don't work very well—alcoholism, drug abuse among parents, child abuse." He adds, "That isn't to imply that we lack responsibility for what we do." He goes on to say, "When you talk about remedies in our society, you have to talk about the fundamental problems that we face—poverty, jobs, the question of values, the school systems, the curricula that don't relate to aptitudes. We ought to be putting more money into counselling, and watching for this kind of thing." He continues, "These kids out here talked about seeing their mother being beaten. *They* were beaten. This rage and hate has to come out sometime. There isn't a lot of hope without some love and some security, something to live by, role models. Not that they haven't any responsibility for themselves, but there's only so much any of us can do; all of us need help."

As he leaves the center, he asks Miss Gittler to find Francis's lawyer and talk to him. Afterward, he says to me, "One of the things that strike you is the hopelessness of some of these situations." He changes the subject briefly, and then comes back to what he's just seen. He talks about the boys, about "the pain and suffering in their hearts." He says, "Take Francis—he's keeping a stiff upper lip, but he's crying inside. That doesn't mean that there aren't some who are no damn good." He mentions something else, and then, returning once more to the boys he has just spoken to, he says, "You know, self-esteem is the whole goddam thing. If they tell you at home you're not worth a damn, and they tell you at school you're no goddam good—at some point you lash back."

We have to fly to Waterloo, and it is two-forty-five; we're a half hour behind schedule and Culver is unhappy about that. He's also tired; in the car on the way to the airport, his eyes start to close.

In Waterloo, Culver visits an armed-services recruiting station. He has a press release ready that says he is "generally encouraged by the progress of the volunteer force thus far in attracting qualified men and women for military service." (The release drafted by his staff had been more enthusiastic, but Culver had toned it down.) The release also says that he is concerned about some recruiting practices. On the way here, he told me that he supports the volunteer force, and does not think that "continuing a forced draft is compatible with a democratic society." He said he thought the argument that the volunteer service cost too much more than the selective-service system is a false one, because Congress had already decided to substantially increase military pay. He said, "And I don't think the argument that it would be Hessians, but black, has been borne out. The draft ended up disproportionately black anyway—the combat troops in Vietnam were virtually all black." One concern that Culver has about the volunteer system is that "the advertising is lousy." He says, "It appeals to everything but patriotism. So they mislead people. They promise them a kind of time they won't have." (At the recruiting center, a brochure entitled "Europe" shows some smiling soldiers in a lovely mountain setting, smiling couples in a café, and so on.) On the way to the recruiting station, he studied a fact sheet providing figures on the size of the services, the percentages of whites and non-whites in them, the number of women, the dropout rates, and other data, and now he gives a television interview, citing many of these figures. That makes three media markets he has covered in one day, talking about a different substantive issue in each of them, demonstrating his practical interest in subjects of real concern—and of his choosing. Actually, there was nothing to keep his interviewers from asking him about the Soviet trials or Andrew Young; they just didn't do it.

Next, Culver talks to a group of representatives of the different armed services and to the regional representative of the company that handles the advertising for the services. He tells them that he is concerned about "people coming in under a false flag—about whether people look at the military as just another job, just another vacation, as opposed to describing it as a duty to one's country," and he adds, "I know it's fashionable to say patriotism is dead. I feel just the opposite. I think we ought to talk about it as a commitment." He also tells the members of the group that he wants them to understand that, as a senator, he gets requests from people who are having problems in the military, or whose relatives are having problems, and that "my role is to respond and refer them to the military." He continues, "But I respect the fact that you have your rules and regulations and standards. The fact that we refer a complaint doesn't necessarily mean we think it's merited, and I'm not reluctant to say that I think the service has responded adequately, that the complaint is not merited." He says, "We're not just coming in and trying to question your decisions. We're just trying to respond to a constituent. And if I don't like your policy, then it's up to me to get a change in the regulations—and if they don't like the new regulations I've got, they can always get rid of me." He asks the representatives of the various services how their recruiting is coming, about specific problems they might have. It's past five now, and it's hot, and he's tired, and, as happens on these trips, the group has prepared more presentations for him than his schedule or his stamina can take. This is their big chance. He listens politely for a while, and then thanks everybody for coming out on a Saturday afternoon. "I just wanted to hear what's on your mind. I want to thank you very much for what you're doing," he says. "It's very important. We're not worth much if we can't get people in the service."

Culver's wife, Ann, and the Culvers' two younger children, Cathy, who is fourteen, and Chet, who is twelve, meet us at the home of Lynn and Henry Cutler, in Waterloo. The Culvers are an athletic family. Ann Culver is a warm, soft-spoken, beautiful woman (blond hair and large blue eyes); she was a United States diving champion and also a North American speed-skating champion, and the children are all seriously involved in sports of one kind or another. In Washington, Ann Culver teaches diving classes.

Lynn Cutler is quite active in Iowa Democratic

politics, and there are a number of photographs of politicians in her downstairs hallway, including several of Jimmy Carter, who attended a party at the Cutlers' during his quest for votes in the 1976 Iowa precinct caucuses. Henry Cutler, a lawyer, acts in the Waterloo Community Playhouse repertory company, and for years he has asked Culver to see one of his performances. Tonight, he has a starring role in "A Funny Thing Happened on the Way to the Forum." So now Culver, tired as he is, stands and talks with a large group that the Cutlers have assembled to see him and to have wine and cheese; he answers their questions, listens to their requests. One of the guests, a man who is involved in Democratic politics, tells me that what Culver has been doing this weekend does not come easily to him. (However Culver may have felt about it, he did it with the same intensity that he brings to the rest of his work.) This man says that he disagrees with criticism of Culver for not doing it more often and says he is pleased that Culver is concentrating on the issues in Washington. He says that he likes Culver's "blunt, bluff style." He continues, "He's natural, he's straight. I like the fullness of his personality." As we talk, I can hear Culver, in another room, telling a story and laughing.

After dinner at the Cutlers', we go to the Waterloo Community Playhouse, where, before the curtain goes up, Culver is introduced to the audience, which applauds appreciatively, and later laughs very hard at a joke in the play about corruption in the Roman Senate—harder, Lynn Cutler tells us, then the audiences did on any other evening. After the play, we drive to the Waterloo airport to fly to McGregor. As our plane crosses the Mississippi River—we will land in Prairie du Chien, Wisconsin, just across the river from McGregor—Culver points it out to me excitedly. Clearly, he can't wait to get home.

8

SUNDAY, JULY 16TH: This peaceful bluff on which Culver has built his Iowa home is about as far as imaginable from his life in Washington—from the pressures, the noise, the phoniness, the speeches, the people always at him. From the table on the porch, where he and his wife and children and I are having breakfast, one looks out on the Mississippi, about five hundred feet below, and across the Mississippi to Wisconsin. There used to be a tower near this spot, from which, it is said, on a clear day—"and if you had very good eyes," Culver adds—one could see four states: Wisconsin, Minnesota, Illinois, and Iowa. Culver has an American flag flying on a promontory overlooking the river. Toward the other end of the porch is some graceful wicker furniture inherited from Ann Culver's family. It is clear that she loves this refuge, too. "Every summer, I look forward to getting out here earlier," she says. (The Culvers also spend Christmas here when they can.) There are a number of pleasure boats out on the river today, and Culver tells me that ordinarily the river is quieter. Ann Culver tells us that the Delta Queen, a sternwheeler that travels to St. Paul, Dubuque, Cincinnati, and New Orleans, among other cities, went by yesterday, and Culver is disappointed that I did not see it. The family is planning a houseboating trip on the river later this summer. This northeast corner of Iowa is shaped in rugged hills—in contrast to the rest of the state, which is flat or gently rolling—because the glacier that levelled much of the land passed this area by. Because of its topography, it is called Little Switzerland.

Today, Culver is dressed in khakis, a sports shirt, and sandals, and he is relaxed and happy. But the enthusiast in him—and also the strong streak of the teacher—comes out as he eagerly tells me about his home and about the history of the area. "You've got to turn me off once I get going on this," he says. The Culvers bought the Heights Hotel, a small, rundown structure, in 1969, and since then they have thoroughly reconditioned it as a residence. "I was invited up here to speak to some First World War veterans the first time I ran for Congress," Culver tells me. "I spoke right from this porch. All the time, I was looking out from this porch at the river, and they were asleep, so we were all thinking of something else. I kept coming back up here to sit here and look. I thought it was the most peaceful place I'd ever seen."

Culver tells of how the explorers Père Jacques Marquette and Louis Joliet reached the upper Mississippi in June of 1673, how "they'd heard about this great river and thought it was the route to China." He tells stories of Marquette and Joliet and the Indians; he has read extensively on the history of exploration, and on a wall he has a replica of a letter written by Joliet. He tells me about the fighting among the French and the British and the Americans over the fur trade in the area; about how the first white settlement was established here at the same time that William Penn founded Philadelphia; about how John Jacob Astor had a fur-trading outpost here. "Very few people appreciate the penetration of early American history into the upper Mississippi," Culver says.

Also on the walls of the house are pictures of old buildings in McGregor. Culver has been one of the leaders in the restoration of the town, which was an important river port in the middle and late nineteenth century and now has a population of about a thousand. And there are pictures of steamboats on the river ("Can you imagine the glory days around here?"); wallboards from an old Iowa City club signed by, among others, Grant Wood, Nicholas Roosevelt, Stephen Vincent Benét, Thomas Hart Benton, and MacKinlay Kantor; antiques he has collected ("Isn't this a great old butcher block?"); and a collection of brass objects from his travels around the world. Culver pulls out of a cabinet some old pamphlets telling the history of the area and reads to me from them, and shows me, in the upstairs hallway, a framed replica of a letter written to him by one of the original hotel's early owners. The letter says, among other things, that Grant Wood spent his honeymoon here. Culver had an artist reproduce the letter, which he has framed along with a reproduction of one of Grant Wood's drawings. Hanging over this is a reproduction of Wood's "American Gothic," and along the same wall are a number of other Wood reproductions. Culver shows me the hand-chiselled mantel over the fireplace and some old pieces of furniture that the Culvers have fixed up. The house itself is beige with white trim and has two and a half stories. The second story is reached by a steel circular staircase that leads up from the living room; the old hotel had only an outdoor staircase. He shows me terrace work that he did around the house, three stones from his great-grandfather's childhood home in Carlisle, Pennsylvania, which he brought out here and put in the wall of the house, crab-apple trees that he planted, even awnings that he carefully selected. "What I love about this place are the history, the physical beauty, the interest and activity of it—the river is alive; it's not like looking at a lake—and the variety of seasons," he says. "I wish you could see it in the fall. I've seen a good bit of the world. I think if someone told me I had a week to live I'd come right here."

Then Culver takes me around to see some of the sights of the area: Pikes Peak State Park, named after Zebulon Pike, who in the early eighteen-hundreds, as a young Army officer, was sent up the Mississippi to survey for suitable military posts and found this place before he travelled west to Colorado. The park overlooks the site where Marquette and Joliet came down the Wisconsin River and entered the Mississippi. At the park, Culver points out a lovely stone house that is a refreshment-and-souvenir stand, and tells me it was built during the W.P.A. era. "Why the hell can't we keep doing things like that?" he says. "Why can't we organize ourselves to do that?" On the way to the park, we drove along what is called the Great River Road, a federal scenic highway. Culver pushed for the scenic-highway designation in the House and in the Senate, so that, he says, "there could be a scenic, uncluttered road overlooking the river, with no hot-dog stands, and with outlooks and places for picnics." He shows me the downtown area of McGregor: antique shops, a winery, restored buildings, including the one he restored, of which he has the painting in his Washington office. It has an ornate black-gold-and-white Victorian metal façade (it was a dull green when Culver bought the building); the courtyard is laid with paving bricks in a herringbone pattern, copied from the brick walk of a Victorian mansion in Prairie du Chien, and is enclosed by a wrought-iron fence that Culver had reproduced from a photograph of a fence he had seen in Wisconsin. He takes me through the building—it is as yet unfinished inside—showing me doors he bought in Mexico, talking of the various ideas he has for finishing it and for how it might be used. He speaks with regret about the fact that there won't be time to show me the town's museum or the Victorian mansion across the river in Prairie du Chien or some Indian burial mounds.

In the afternoon, the Culver family and their dog and I go out on the Mississippi in a pontoon boat. Ann Culver has prepared some quiches. The river is high from the rains—too high for a planned picnic on a sandbar. Sheer cliffs rise on either side. From time to time, a barge carrying goods someplace down the river comes along, having just passed through a lock-and-dam system built by the Corps of Engineers. (Culver voted this year to charge the waterway users a fee, though there was heavy pressure against such a move by significant economic interests in his state. In the boat this afternoon, he says, "You know, we subsidize the railroads, we subsidize the airlines, we subsidize the truckers, we subsidize the shippers. How do we know what works and who needs what?") Sometimes he pilots the boat—holding a cigar in his mouth and wearing a dark-blue cap he brought back from China—and sometimes he relaxes while his son pilots it; sometimes he chats, and sometimes he is silent, looking at the scenery. He points out special sights—the beauty of a bridge, the colors on a hillside. He talks about his McGregor house: "It's the greatest thing I ever did—for the kids, the family, and for me. For me, there's the relaxation, the interest, and"—he pauses—"the sanity. You know, I can get away here and get all absorbed in thinking about what kinds of awnings to put up, in having someone come over and discuss the terracing."

It's clearly a wrench for Culver to leave McGregor this evening, but he must fly from Prairie du Chien to Dubuque and from there to Chicago in order to make a speech to the Outdoor Advertising Association of America tomorrow morning. He isn't enthusiastic about making the speech, but it helps him supplement his income. The way our national legislators are compensated is very hard on those who, like Culver, are not wealthy, and popular sentiment is making it harder. Senators are paid a salary of fifty-seven thousand five hundred dollars a year, which, after taxes, leaves someone like Culver with between thirty and forty thousand dollars. Currently, they are also allowed to earn up to twenty-five thousand dollars in honorariums, and, in addition, other income from business and the practice of law, but next year their total annual outside earnings, with minor exceptions, will be limited to eight thousand six hundred and twenty-five dollars. (After taxes, they will have only about half those amounts.) Unearned income—income from trusts, stocks, and bonds—is not counted, and therefore people who have family fortunes or who made a great deal of money before being elected to the Senate do not have a problem. The requirements for financial statements this year are so vague that only seventeen senators listed themselves as millionaires, while it has been reliably estimated that the actual figure is closer to over a third of the Senate, and that a substantial number more have considerable wealth. It is very difficult for those who, like Culver, want to play it straight—who have avoided such things as practicing law on the side or being in some way on the take. Senators must maintain two homes—one in Washington and one in their state;

if they have children (and Culver has four), they must consider how they will put them through college. (Walter Mondale, also not a wealthy man, has joked that he took the Vice Presidency for the money.)

As Culver gets increasingly near Chicago this evening, he gradually gets wound back up for returning to Washington tomorrow and managing the debate on the endangered-species bill. A representative of the Outdoor Advertising Association who meets us at the airport and takes us into town by limousine (Culver hates limousines) cannot tell him what time he is to speak, or where, or whether he will be able to make an early plane to Washington. Culver doesn't explode, but it is clear that he is on the verge.

9

MONDAY, JULY 17TH: Culver has made his speech and caught the ten-o'clock plane to Washington—the one he hoped to catch—and now, on the plane, he studies a thick black notebook that his staff has put together for the endangered-species debate. The morning papers indicate that the Senate may be caught up in a small filibuster on an energy bill, and this would mean that Culver's bill might not come up today after all. But he can't know now. "That's always the way," he says. "All the uncertainty. You don't know what's coming up when. But you have to be ready." He studies the notebook, making marginal notes and questions. The intensity has returned. He explains the "cross fire" that he is worried about: that the more he stresses, in rebutting Nelson, the fact that his proposal will not dilute the Endangered Species Act, the more the people who oppose the act as it stands will try to weaken or kill his proposal, or the act itself; on the other hand, the more he stresses, in rebutting those who want to weaken the act, the fact that his proposal makes it more flexible, the more the environmentalists will be opposed.

Culver reaches his office shortly after one o'clock and is told that the endangered-species bill will come up sometime between four and six o'clock, and that this afternoon there will be only opening statements, with the real debate and the offering of amendments to begin tomorrow. He asks Dick Oshlo to call a man he saw at the Cutlers' in Waterloo who wanted some information on pollution problems. He gives Pat Sarcone a copy of the program of "A Funny Thing Happened on the Way to the Forum" and suggests that she draft a letter for him to send to each of the members of the cast, telling them how much he and his family enjoyed the play, and also asks her to draft letters to the Cutlers, to John Chrystal, and to some of the other people he saw over the weekend. After he is given mail and memos that have accumulated, he tells the staff a couple of stories from the trip, and asks them if anything else has come up. Pat Sarcone tells him that he has been invited to a breakfast meeting at the White House at eight o'clock on Wednesday with the President, Defense Secretary Harold Brown, Clark Clifford—a Washington attorney who has been advising the Administration on the Cyprus dispute—and Warren Christopher, the Deputy Secretary of State, on the question of lifting the embargo on the sale of arms to Turkey. Culver says that he will go.

"Senator," Dick Oshlo says, "I think you should meet with Howard Baker this afternoon." The idea is to go over a couple of questions of strategy with Baker, co-sponsor of Culver's compromise. Oshlo also tells him that Nelson wants to meet with him and that the National Audubon Society has endorsed Culver's proposal. Oshlo says that he now thinks that Nelson's threat to move to kill Culver's proposal is a bluff—that what Nelson really wants is for Culver to accept some minor amendments. Oshlo goes over some of the amendments that Nelson is expected to propose; Culver says he can't accept some of them, raises questions about some others, suggests compromises.

Culver tells Oshlo that what he wants to do this afternoon is read some of his opening statement and put the rest in the *Congressional Record*, saving time he has been given for general debate, under the unanimous-consent agreement on the terms of the floor consideration of this bill, and using it for the debate on amendments. (Over the weekend, we talked about the controversy over the fact that members of Congress put statements in the *Record* which they do not deliver. Under a recent change, statements that are not delivered at all are preceded by large black dots, but statements that are read in part can still appear as if they had been read in their entirety. A few members insist on reading their entire statements, in the interests of purity. "I put statements in the *Record*," Culver said. "It's no big deal. I just put my position down. It's there for people to see. After all, what's the point in taking everyone's time and boring everyone by reading it?") Culver tells Oshlo that the opening statement that has been prepared for him needs to be revised. Oshlo says that it already has been. Culver continues, "Ask them to come up with the best answers to each argument, with specificity. Some of the background material has some pretty good information that hasn't been used. Pull together the best arguments from the basic materials. Nelson's going to get up and say that there have been forty-five hundred consultations where questions have arisen over whether a project will harm an endangered species, and there's been only one problem." Culver is referring to consultations that the Endangered Species Act requires between the agencies that are to build a project and the Fish and Wildlife Service, which administers the act, and to the one instance in which a project had to be stopped—the ruling by the Supreme Court in June that the construction of the Tellico Dam, in Tennessee, had to cease because it threatened the existence of the snail darter.

He continues, "We should be able to point out that the great majority of those consultations involved telephone conversations and didn't represent real problems. We should point out that the number of species listed as endangered is going up, so we're going to have twenty thousand consultations in 1979 alone. We should say how many endangered species were listed in 1973 and how many this year and what the percentage increase is. We should have a very specific, step-by-step explanation of how the new process would work. Some of that is ambiguous in the working papers." Then he asks some precise questions about the process. All this is a result of his reading on the plane. "We have to clarify these things," he says. "I just think we've got to be able to walk through that process very tight. The problem I sense in the material I have here is that it's intellectually flabby—it's just scattered all over. It says here that more than one governor might be involved. What if the governors can't agree? I think we've got to have all the facts on one card. I mean, we've got a hell of a lot of numbers floating around here."

Culver goes on, "The other thing I want to get straight is the money. Why do we need more money for that new commission?" He is referring to the interagency committee that his proposal would establish to resolve disputes under the Endangered Species Act. He continues, "You know, every time we turn around we're asking for another commission. We're going to get asked what the money is for, how many high-level employees the committee will have, what their work load will be. We've got to anticipate those questions." He asks Oshlo some more questions, and says, "O.K., I want to see all that typed out." Oshlo tells him that Gary Hart and John Chafee, both of them members of the Environment and Public Works Committee and strong environmentalists, are going to stick with him. Culver is pleased. Oshlo says that the prospect of Nelson's moving to kill the Culver compromise has alarmed some of the environmental groups—if it succeeded, it would leave the old act intact and so more vulnerable to its opponents—and that they have gone to work to shore up support for the compromise.

At two-twenty, Culver calls the Democratic cloakroom to see what the legislative situation is, and then he goes over his schedule with Jim Larew—giving him responses to invitations and to requests for appointments that have come in (he says he'll try to meet today with Iowa's two representatives to Boys Nation and go to a reception for Mrs. Anatoly Shcharansky, the wife of the Soviet dissident who was recently convicted of treason, but that he might not be able to do either one, because he'll be managing the bill)—and reads some more material on endangered species.

Shortly after three o'clock, he gets ready to go to meet with Baker and with staff members of both senators. As Culver is about to leave for Baker's office, Fred Holborn, one of Culver's senior assistants, comes in and, smiling, tells him that he must have done great work at the Linn County Juvenile Detention Center—that three of the young men escaped the day after we were there. Culver laughs, and says, "I'm sitting there like Father Flanagan, and the next thing is they're going over the wall."

I ask him if he is concerned that people will say that this shows he is "just another bleeding heart."

He is silent for a moment, and then says, "Hell, I didn't build the place." Then he says, "Those kids' lives are just as bad as when they went in.

They aren't going to change in a couple of days—if ever."

At eight minutes past four, on the Senate floor, Culver calls up S. 2899, the Endangered Species Act Amendments of 1978. He is standing behind the desk where bill managers are stationed—in the front row, just to the left of the center aisle. Malcolm Wallop, who, as the ranking minority member of Culver's subcommittee, will manage the bill for the Republican side, but who supports Culver's proposal, is at the desk on the opposite side of the aisle. George Jacobson and Kathi Korpon, Culver's staff aides for matters before the Environment and Public Works Committee, are seated beside Culver. Because Culver is managing the bill and must frequently refer to notes, he uses one of the small lecterns that senators sometimes put on top of their desks when they speak. Culver reads, fairly routinely, from his opening statement. His purpose now is simply to establish some legislative history. There are few senators on the floor; these opening moves are just shadowboxing. The real debate begins tomorrow. Under the unanimous-consent agreement for this bill, there will be two hours for general debate—time that will be equally divided between the majority and the minority. In addition, an hour and a half will be devoted to debate on an amendment to be offered by John Stennis to weaken the bill—equally divided between proponents and opponents—and a half hour for debate on each of the other amendments, also equally divided. Stennis was given extra time because he was until recently chairman of the Public Works Subcommittee of the Appropriations Committee (and is its ranking member) and, in general, is an important senator, and he had submitted the major amendment against the bill. Nelson is still asking for more time for his amendment to kill Culver's compromise, and Culver is concerned that other members who have amendments will also want more time, and then the unanimous-consent agreement under which the bill is being debated will come undone. (Anyway, one can always gain more time by offering an amendment to an amendment.)

Now Culver, reading his statement, says, "The Endangered Species Act was a recognition—and a woefully late one—that our developmental activities were responsible for destroying forms of life which were present as a result of processes which began with the first appearance of life on earth three and a half billion years ago." He talks about the "sharp acceleration in the rate of extinction, to the point where the natural process may be increased by a factor of hundreds or even thousands." Then he explains the problem that has arisen under the act, which requires that "all federal agencies undertake necessary precautions to assure that actions or projects authorized, funded, or carried out by them do not jeopardize the continued existence of an endangered species or its critical habitat." He points out that this provision has prevented the completion of the Tellico Dam, and he adds that "it appears likely that a growing number of other projects will not be completed because of this section." He says his subcommittee has been told that the Fish and Wildlife Service sometimes refrains from putting a species on the endangered list for fear that doing so might provoke a member of Congress to vote against the act. He explains what his amendment to the act would do: establish an Endangered Species Committee, to be composed of seven public officials, including the heads of six federal agencies and the governor of the state affected by the specific conflict, to arbitrate conflicts that arise over whether projects should be completed. He points out that the proposal was approved unanimously by the Environment and Public Works Committee, and says that "we are satisfied that it does preserve the integrity of the Endangered Species Act and yet provides the flexibility which will be needed in the coming years." This is not a real Culver speech—that will come tomorrow. He adds, returning to a theme that runs through much of his thinking, "Most importantly, it is an attempt to get ahead of foreseeable problems and be prepared for them in a rational way."

Wallop speaks, complimenting Culver, whereupon Culver rises and says that he was remiss in not complimenting Wallop. Nelson comes over to Culver while Wallop is talking, and asks if Culver will accept any of his amendments. Culver says that he, Baker, and Wallop discussed the matter in Baker's office but didn't reach any decisions. Then Nelson asks him about the time problem. Culver would like to establish a situation in which Nelson would feel that he has had time to have his objections to the compromise aired and would then withdraw his amendment to kill it, whereupon Culver would accept some of Nelson's minor amendments. In the course of these discussions, Culver and Nelson kid around. They oppose each other here, but Culver is going to the Nelson's home for dinner tomorrow evening. "I never thought you'd do it to me, Gaylord," Culver says. He sits behind the desk, looking like a schoolboy in a classroom. Some senators—Henry Jackson, and Claiborne Pell, Democrat of Rhode Island—come along to discuss with him amendments they want to offer. Jackson and Culver could well end up in a brutal battle over a SALT treaty, and both men must know it, but now Jackson has his arm around Culver and the two of them are smiling. There is a lot of arm-grabbing, shoulder-hugging, and backslapping in the Senate; it is noticeable that Culver, though he is one of the friendliest of senators, does less of this business than many of the others.

William Scott is speaking. Scott has a number of amendments to weaken the bill. There is a kind of expectancy when Scott speaks: people figure he can be counted on to say something inadvertently amusing. "One can only be thankful that dinosaurs don't exist today," Scott says.

Nelson speaks, saying, "We are left with the Tellico project as the sole basis for a sweeping attack on this landmark legislation."

Shortly after five-thirty, this preliminary debate is ended. Culver has yielded his colleagues as little of his hour for general debate as he could, within the bounds of Senate courtesy; Wallop, too, has saved as much time as possible. They figure that they may need this time to oppose some amendments.

Culver runs into Nelson at the subway from the Capitol back to the Senate office buildings. Nelson says to Culver, "You'll be there tomorrow night?"

Culver replies, laughing, "That depends on how acrimonious the debate is."

At the end of the day, Culver gives his staff some more assignments and gathers some more materials to study for tomorrow's debate. He also tells me that he has just learned from Charles Stevenson that the C.I.A. has agreed to declassify and release the report by the intelligence community on Soviet civil defense that Culver has been urging it to release for two years, and that he plans to hold a press conference on it on Wednesday. Tonight, he wants to prepare for his own speech tomorrow and to think through his strategy on the amendments. He tells me, "I think it's important to win the first one in a situation like this, so that the committee stays in control. Stennis has a major amendment; Nelson has a major amendment; others have amendments. So the question is which would be the best one for us to have brought up first. I haven't figured that out yet. Of course, if Nelson wins, it's all over for us."

10

TUESDAY, JULY 18TH: At nine-thirty, Culver is working in Room 244, a nicely furnished conference room near the Senate floor, which is part of the office complex of Secretary of the Senate Stanley Kimmitt. George Jacobson is sitting beside him, hard at work making notes on a yellow legal pad. Culver has a large number of papers and documents spread before him. Beginning early this morning, Culver has studied the endangered-species material, and has had breakfast in the Senate dining room with Dick Oshlo, George Jacobson, Kathi Korpon, and Fred Holborn. At eight-thirty, the group adjourned to this room. Culver gave the various members of his staff more assignments, talked over with them which of the various pending amendments might be acceptable, and asked them to get more information on some of the amendments.

He tells me now, "The major thing is to try to get quality rather than quantity ready. It's like a college exam, and there's a C-plus answer, where you're spewing back information that you've read in the books and there is no evidence you've really digested it." He continues, switching metaphors,

"The challenge here is to get the material through the eye of the needle—to match the information with the specific amendments and to organize it. I expressed my displeasure with the limitations of the material that was here. It was all spread out in a disjointed way. It's a question of organizing the material and anticipating the debating points you're going to need. George, here, is working on a point-by-point rebuttal to Nelson. I've asked him to list Nelson's best arguments on one side of the page and our best arguments on the other." Culver now has fact sheets about the amendments, and about the sequence of events under the new process he is proposing. He has had the black notebook reorganized. "There are about thirty amendments that will be offered that we know of," he explains. "So the idea is to get them clustered in the notebook by subject, because we'll be in the middle—having things coming at us from right and left." He tells me that in the discussions he and his staff had earlier this morning "it was generally concluded that the best approach would be to have the Stennis amendment brought up first, and I'll informally ask the chair to recognize him first—because so many of the arguments I will use against Nelson about how our amendment will strengthen the Endangered Species Act could then be used by Stennis and company to show why our proposal should be weakened. So if I make a major argument against Stennis and defeat him, then I can take on Nelson and make the other arguments at that point."

Culver says that what he will do now is study the fact sheets that the staff has prepared for him on all the amendments that can be expected to come up. He has asked Fred Holborn to find some quotations for him to use in the debate. Culver wants the specific wording of one by Oliver Wendell Holmes, Jr., which he particularly likes: "All rights tend to declare themselves absolute to their logical extreme. Yet all in fact are limited by the neighborhood of principles of policy which are other than those on which the particular right is founded. . . ." Kathi Korpon is scouting around for answers to a number of new questions he has raised. He has a great deal of material to absorb—quickly. This will be the largest and most complex piece of legislation he has managed in the Senate. He wants to do well not only because that is in his own nature but also because of the nature of the Senate. It is a competitive place—made up of people whose competitiveness got them there to begin with. Culver is well aware that through one's performance the esteem of one's colleagues and one's position in the pecking order—and future influence—are established. And even within this context Culver—the former football star—is one of the more competitive people.

As Culver sits at the table, he outlines on a yellow legal pad the arguments he wants to make in his opening speech. He says, "I want to get down what I'll be talking about in a more general way than I did yesterday—about the whole mystery of the universe, and the process of extinction, and what's natural and what's unnatural, and what's the best way to organize ourselves, given the mysterious nature of these things, the best way to try to cope. I want to explain in simple, lay terms what we're trying to accomplish with our proposal." He has been looking through some general articles on the subject, and has brought in a book, "The Challenge of Man's Future," by Harrison Brown. "Gaylord Nelson gave this to me," he says. "It was published in 1954, and it triggered his interest in these questions. It might be useful to turn it back on him."

The Senate has taken time out from the debate on the endangered-species bill to consider a nomination to the Small Business Administration. Culver says, "I just hope the opponents of the nomination are sufficiently indignant to keep the debate going until at least two o'clock." (He has received a memorandum from his staff on the S.B.A. nomination to look over before he votes on it.)

Culver and Jacobson tell me that they still are not sure whether various environmental groups will back Culver or Nelson. "It's not an atypical situation," Culver says. "You have the private views of the leaders versus organizational constituency purism—the leaders don't communicate the political realities." This is a common phenomenon in Washington: the leaders or representatives of an interest group may understand the political "realities" but take an uncompromising public stand, not only as a bargaining position but also as a way of protecting themselves with their own constituencies. These people are paid to wring as much as possible out of the government on behalf of their clients, to make the worst case analysis of the alternatives to what they seek. They recognize that they are subject to challenge from within the ranks on the charge that they were not sufficiently true to the organization's professed goals, that they "sold out." In the process, they can end up preventing a resolution of a conflict, and thus fail to represent their groups' true interests. Culver continues, "And the developers are against the act. It's the old cross fire. You don't have the choice of having a utopian king work these things out. Is Congress going to do it? Is some agency going to do it? Is the President going to do it? That's what we have to decide—how to work out these conflicts."

Culver still does not know whether Nelson is going to put the proposal to kill Culver's compromise to a vote. He explains to me that the environmental groups might not want such a vote: if they see that it might lose by a substantial margin, and then if the House weakens the Endangered Species Act, Culver will not have much bargaining power in the ensuing Senate-House conference to try to strengthen the act—which some of the provisions of his proposal would do. Moreover, if the Nelson amendment should be soundly defeated, that would indicate political weakness on the part of the environmental groups.

At eleven o'clock, Culver steps into the next room for a cup of coffee, and on his return he says that he has just learned from Kimmitt that the vote on the S.B.A. nomination will take place at twelve-thirty, and that he will have to be ready to resume the debate on the endangered-species bill right after that. The Environment and Public Works Committee's Environmental Pollution Subcommittee, on which Culver sits, is holding a meeting now. One of Culver's aides is covering it for him and will let him know if he is needed there for any votes. The Senate-House conference on the military-procurement bill, to which Culver, in committee and last week on the Senate floor, succeeded in attaching some amendments, including the one designed to make the large aircraft carrier provided for in the bill the last one, will begin this afternoon, and Charles Stevenson will cover that for him. Now Culver puts his hands on his forehead, concentrates very hard, and from time to time makes notes on the yellow pad. It is as if he were a lawyer preparing a very important argument. Occasionally, he asks Jacobson a question; for example, exactly how to define a "gene pool." His face grows redder as he applies pressure on himself. He asks Jacobson to be sure he has handy the examples of problems in working out conflicts over a project, and asks him, "What is the best answer to the argument that this act has had a five-year shakedown cruise and now there is a heightened sensitivity to avoiding conflict, and therefore our amendment is premature?"

Jacobson replies, "Senator, there is no way

around the problem that a project could be well along and they will find a species in trouble."

He asks Jacobson to be sure to have a list of species that could be jeopardized by Stennis's amendment. As he studies the material, he finds a mistake in one of the fact sheets he has been given ("God, you've got to proofread this stuff," he says) and finds a gap in the chronology he has requested on how his proposal would work. He is clearly perturbed.

All this began as a duty for Culver: he heads the Resource Protection Subcommittee; the Endangered Species Act needed to be reauthorized, because otherwise it would expire this fall. In taking up the bill, Culver found himself amid highly charged competing interests: the environmentalists, who wanted to preserve the act, and the builders (who include a large number of business and political interests), who wanted to weaken it. Both sides were pursuing serious purposes. Culver took on the job of trying to mediate, to construct a world in which both could function. Moreover, he had to find a solution at a time when there was an increasingly strong public mood against government programs—particularly programs such as this, which impose regulations, can increase costs, and are seen to impede "progress." Almost by chance, he ended up grappling with an issue much larger than the particulars of the bill before him: the question of finding mechanisms for resolving the increasing number of conflicts between competing interests in our society. That is what this issue is really about. Typically, Culver worked toward a solution that could win a consensus in the committee, and it has come to the Senate floor with the committee's unanimous approval. Now he must try to preserve the compromise he has wrought.

At noon, Steve Rapp phones and tells Culver

that in fifteen minutes the Judiciary Committee will vote on Birch Bayh's bill, giving the Attorney General the authority to sue, and to intervene in suits, to protect the rights of people in non-federal institutions—which was put over from the meeting last week—and that Culver's vote is needed. Culver gathers up some of the papers he has been working on and heads for the Dirksen Office Building. On the subway, Culver talks briefly to a reporter from the Des Moines *Register.* Rapp meets Culver as he reaches the committee room, briefs him on where things stand, and hands him some memorandums about the Bayh bill, amendments to it, and other matters before the committee. In the course of the meeting, Culver alternately studies the memorandums and the endangered-species material, making more marginal notes, and casts his votes. Bayh's bill is approved.

At twelve-forty, as the Judiciary Committee meeting is about to end, the buzzers sound, signalling a roll-call vote on the S.B.A. nomination. Culver collects his material to go to the floor, and as he makes his way there he is met by a constituent, a woman who has been a supporter.

"How are you?" Culver says. "Great to see you!"

She walks along with him and he chats with her as if there were nothing else on his mind.

"If you want anything in Dubuque, holler," she says as she leaves him.

"Thanks," Culver says, smiling. "You're sweet."

Culver goes to the floor to vote and then returns to Kimmitt's office, where Fred Holborn, Dick Oshlo, and Kathi Korpon have rejoined George Jacobson. "All right, what's up?" he asks. Holborn hands him some cards with quotations on them. Culver reads one aloud. " 'A man who prides himself upon acting upon principle is likely to be a man who insists upon having his own way without learning from experience what is the better way.' John Dewey. That's great," Culver says, and he adds, smiling, "Hate to do it to you, Gaylord." He has a lot to do now, but he's interested in the quotations. He reads another one aloud—this one also by Holmes—"To have doubted one's own first principles is the mark of a civilized man." Other staff members give him more memorandums, and he discusses with them which Nelson amendments they might accept, and the group agrees that it still seems best to begin with the Stennis amendment. "I'd better get out there now and make sure Stennis is the lead," Culver says.

At one o'clock, Stennis calls up his amendment. Culver is sitting in his chair in the front row. Stennis's amendment would exempt from the Endangered Species Act any projects that are half completed, or that had been contracted for at the time the act became law, in 1973. It would also allow the agency in charge of the project to determine whether it should be completed. The amendment is supported by the United States Chamber of Commerce and the National Forest Products Association. As Stennis argues for his amendment, Culver listens; thinks; sorts the materials before him; talks with Jacobson, who is sitting beside him; makes more notes; studies his yellow sheets. Stennis argues that the Tellico Dam had been ninety per cent complete, and about a hundred million dollars had been spent on it, when it was halted. He points out that a right-of-way for a highway that was being built in Mississippi had to be rerouted because it was going to go through the habitat of the sandhill crane—"a rather attractive-looking bird with a red top notch." He says that forty-six cranes were involved, and explains that to deal with that problem cost two years and four million dollars, and that eighteen million two hundred thousand dollars more was spent to find an additional habitat for those birds—for a total, Stennis says, of around four hundred and eighty thousand dollars per crane. One of the largest new public-works projects, the Tennessee-Tombigbee water project, goes through Mississippi and might encounter several endangered species. As Stennis speaks, Culver catches him in a small mistake and politely asks him to yield for a correction. Stennis thanks him for the correction.

At one-twenty-three, Culver rises to speak, ostensibly in opposition to Stennis's amendment but actually to address himself also to what he knows that Nelson is going to argue. His yellow pages are on the stand in front of him. For his speech today, in contrast to the one he made last week in behalf of his aircraft-carrier amendment, he uses a lapel microphone. It is not that he needs one to be heard but that the lapel microphones at the senators' desks are attached to the speaker system by which the debates are broadcast back to the Senate offices, and some offices complained last week that they could not hear his speech on the carrier amendment. "Mr. President," Culver says, starting at the heart of the matter, "today, in 1978, the members of any elected representative body, as well as public officials and those chosen for leadership responsibilities anywhere throughout the world, are increasingly challenged, intimidated, and, in fact, frustrated by the ever-increasing complexity and enormity of the public-policy problems that they are called upon to address."

He says, "Our resources are not infinite but finite . . . our margin of error is no longer what it was at an earlier day. The consequences of our own fallibility are much more serious in their implication to perhaps even the survival of human life through decisions of each and every one of us individually and collectively as a body." Warming up, his voice rising, he says, "In my judgment, no issue—no issue—more starkly poses that situation than the one that we are addressing ourselves to today, because this question goes to some of the most difficult, unfathomable questions that have always confronted mankind." He says, "They go to the nature of our universe. They go to the nature of our ecosystems, and our biosphere. They go to basic questions of 'What does it all mean.'" He quotes from Winston Churchill and from a Nigerian chieftain. He talks about the cycles of life and death—"whether we speak of mankind, whether we speak of animals, whether we speak of the Furbish lousewort." (The Furbish lousewort is a wild flower that was found in Maine in the path of a proposed hydroelectric project. Culver knows that the name has a funny ring to it.) He gives figures on the increasingly rapid rate by which species are extinguished. He says that, of the two million species of plant and animal life in the world, "biologists estimate some two hundred thousand, *two hundred thousand*"—and his voice booms through the chamber—"may be endangered or rare today." He is addressing himself to Nelson and the environmentalists, showing that he shares their concerns. He refers only infrequently to his notes. He is doing what he prefers to do when he speaks, and what gives him his reputation as one of the most effective orators in the Senate—winging it, on the basis of having studied and thought through and organized the arguments he wants to make.

He talks about the things that have contributed to the extinction of species: commercial hunting and fishing, industrial poisons, the destruction of our forests, the alteration of our water tables—"and, yes, even our shopping centers and our suburban development." He has worked himself into a passion now. His face is red. He shouts as he says, "What is the responsibility of those of us who have an obligation, as stewards of this land during our own short cycle on this earth, before we, too, are extinct? What is our responsibility to those generations yet unborn, and why should we be concerned about toxic pollutants in the air and in the water? What difference does it make? Why should we be concerned about it? It may cost us. We may waste ten million dollars in appropriations. We may have to stop a dam. We may have to stop a highway. We may have to alter the course of a flood-control project. What difference does it make?" He goes on, at full steam now, and, referring to Stennis, he says, "Mr. President, as the distinguished Senator from Mississippi has said, it does on the surface seem stupid to save something like a snail darter, some crazy bat, some crayfish, something called a Furbish lousewort. So you may ask, when you are talking about Tellico and a hundred and seventeen million dollars, Why worry about the snail darter? When push comes to shove, who should win? Which species has the votes in the next election?"

Then he answers his own question. "Aside from aesthetic or ethical considerations, aside from the understandable and natural desire to have diversity and beauty in our world and in our environment, and aside from the continued preservation and existence of these rare and exotic species, it is also true, in my judgment, that we have the ethical and moral responsibility to pass on to future generations, in as pristine a state as possible, what we in turn have inherited, and to increase our knowledge, our awareness, and our sophistication in making discriminating determinations that are informed as to who lives and who dies and what are the consequences." He doesn't address himself specifically to the Stennis amendment; his plan is to have Wallop, a conservative, do that. His major purpose now is to "crowd" Nelson, as he has put it, by talking about the larger points at issue and demonstrating his own concern for the species. From time to time, his husky voice gets hoarse. He points out that there are six hundred species that are designated rare and endangered and another two thousand that are waiting to go on the list. He says that, while Tellico is the most celebrated case, there are at least twelve other major projects over which conflicts have yet to be resolved.

Nelson interrupts to state that he has received a letter from the Fish and Wildlife Service saying that it does not foresee any problem with these twelve cases.

Culver has anticipated this, and he tells Nelson that he has his own letter from the Service, "which I think puts a little different slant on things." He doesn't stick with the point; he doesn't want to get into this now. He returns to one of his recurring themes. "The Congress," he says, "is always being criticized for not getting out ahead of problems, for not anticipating, for not positioning ourselves so we can responsibly and rationally deal with the problems before we are blind-sided and overwhelmed by events." He points out that there have been forty-five hundred consultations between federal agencies in charge of projects and the Fish and Wildlife Service in the last five years, and says it is estimated that there will be twenty thousand consultations in the next year alone, and that "the potential for conflict is inevitable and unavoidable." He says, "Mr. President, we have proposed this mechanism, which in my judgment represents the most responsible and rational balancing of interests. . . . I say, as one who is fervently and devotedly committed to the most powerful protection of our environment and the need to preserve and protect these species, that it does not defy our power of reason to develop a mechanism which, in my judgment, gives us the flexibility we need, and gives it within a context that insulates it from the political pressures that inevitably are going to overpower any other approach."

It is now one-forty-five, and Culver is going strong, but the Senate is scheduled to take up a conference report (a report on a bill that has been passed by both chambers and has been negotiated and approved by conferees representing the Senate and the House) at this time, and so he stops. He sits down, wipes his brow with a handkerchief, and drinks from a glass of water on his desk. During the roll-call vote on the report, he talks with Nelson and with James Sasser, Democrat of Tennessee. He is arranging for Sasser to get some statements on record which deal with the politics of the endangered-species issue in Tennessee. Then Culver comes off the Senate floor, perspiring, and, as is his wont, he questions his performance. "Did I go on too long?" he asks someone. "Was it all right?" He goes to the cloakroom briefly to talk with his staff members about what will be coming up in the course of the afternoon. He does not take time for lunch, and returns to the Senate floor.

After the debate is resumed, Jake Garn, Republican of Utah, who is a conservative, speaks in behalf of the Stennis amendment. He talks about Culver's speech: "In his usual eloquent, articulate manner and with great moral fervor, he interjected such morality into this debate that I feel almost ashamed to rise and offer any changes whatsoever to this great act." He continues, "Nevertheless, I have overcome that."

Culver smiles. He and Garn serve on the Armed Services Committee together, and though they agree on almost nothing, they have an amiable relationship. Garn complains about putting "the rights of a Furbish lousewort over the rights of man." While he speaks, Culver goes over his notes and his quotation cards, and speaks to Gary Hart and to James Pearson, Republican of Kansas.

Then, while Wallop speaks against the Stennis amendment, Culver listens carefully—out of courtesy but also to make sure that all the points are covered. He has told me that when one manages a bill it is essential to watch all the time—for mistakes on the part of allies, for someone who might get the floor and offer a suprise amendment. He carefully doles out time for others to speak.

Then Culver briefly argues against Stennis's amendment. He says that it would "eviscerate" the Endangered Species Act, and he refers to the list, which he has asked his staff to obtain, of the projects that were initiated before 1973 and would be exempted under Stennis's amendment, saying there are roughly six hundred and fifty of them. And then a roll-call vote is taken on Stennis's amendment.

During the vote, Culver "works the floor." He stands at the front, at a desk where a clerk has written a short description of Stennis's amendment, and, as his colleagues file in and come to see what the amendment is, he talks to them about it. He has already seen to it that the description is accurate—sometimes, because the descriptions are so brief, they can be misleading. "It's very important to stay on top of your vote," he has told me. "People may have told them something about what the vote is on when they came in the door and they may have more questions."

During the roll-call vote, Robert Byrd comes up to Culver and tells him that he thinks he will support Stennis. Later, he comes back, puts his hand on Culver's shoulder, and says, "I'll vote with you, but there's something I want to talk to you about."

At this point, it is clear that the Stennis amendment is going down to defeat. Culver smiles, and replies, "Well, not right now, Bob. It looks like Stennis is going to get about twenty votes on this. I'll talk to you when I really need you."

Byrd, a dour man who does not laugh very

much, laughs, and says, "That's so good I'll give you one." And he votes against Stennis.

The Stennis amendment is defeated, twenty-two to seventy-six. The first part of Culver's strategy has worked.

Culver's intention is to accept as many amendments as he can without undermining the purposes of the bill, in order to build the broadest possible consensus behind it. He signals to the presiding officer who should be recognized, thus keeping control of the sequence in which things happen. Now he accepts a minor amendment by Pell and two minor amendments by Nelson. While this is taking place, a representative of an organization called Monitor, a consortium of conservation, environmental, and animal-welfare groups, tells me that there are several other amendments it wants, and that "we are with Nelson all the way." He claims that the Audubon Society "wavered" toward Culver but is now headed back toward support of Nelson.

At four-forty-five, Nelson, speaking from behind his desk, at the rear of the chamber, calls up his amendment to strike the Culver compromise and leave the Endangered Species Act intact. Nelson, ribbing Culver, says, "I have been assuming all afternoon, after listening to that magnificent speech, that at some stage the Senator from Iowa . . . would be so persuaded by what he said that he would get up and withdraw his amendment to the Endangered Species Act. Perhaps the distinguished Senator from Iowa intends to do that at some later moment."

Culver laughs, and rises and asks if Nelson will yield, and Nelson does. Culver says, "I just hope he is not holding his breath until that opportunity presents itself."

Nelson replies, "No, I had not been holding my breath, but I had been waiting breathlessly." He goes on, "I have not before heard, in any forum, a more magnificent defense of this law. . . . I just wanted to endorse what the Senator said and add to his speech just a few words in support of what really adds up to a compelling argument why the law ought to be left alone." And then he makes the arguments that Culver has anticipated: that the act has worked well, that only one project, the Tellico Dam, has been stopped—and he adds that it should not have been begun in the first place.

While Nelson speaks, Culver goes to work on his rebuttal. He asks Nelson to yield again, and inquires what Nelson is worried about "if this act has worked so wonderfully for the last four years." He adds, "Clearly, by his assessment of the situation the committee will never have any work to do, and next year will come back to us and say, 'We tried but couldn't even spend that money, because there were no conflicts.' . . . So I would wait to worry. I would wait to worry."

Nelson says that he worries that the Culver proposal "punches a big hole in a very good law" and authorizes a group of people to decide to destroy a species.

Nelson has run out of time, and Culver offers a technical amendment (to change the word "procure" to "obtain"), in order to give Nelson a chance to go on. He has had several such amendments prepared for this sort of contingency. He hopes that if he gives Nelson ample time to make his case Nelson will be satisfied and withdraw his amendment.

Now Howard Baker asks Nelson to yield. Although Baker is co-sponsor of Culver's amendment, he has taken little part in the debate, and his appearance is brief. He makes an argument for providing flexibility in the law.

It is after five o'clock now, and Culver is clearly wearying. After Nelson has spoken for a while, they get into a snappish exchange over how much time each has consumed in the debate—a moment of tension between friends, each of whom is trying hard to make his case and is under strain. Moreover, as is not always the case in Senate debates, both men are arguing from deep beliefs. The debate on Nelson's proposal was to have been briefer, but both men have been drawn into it by their beliefs. Culver's staff has told him that there is reason to believe that Nelson might withdraw his amendment once it has been debated, but Culver can't be sure that he will. And if tempers get out of hand anything can happen. The moment passes, however, and Culver says that he will arrange for Nelson to get as much time to speak as he needs.

After a while, Culver rises to speak against Nelson's amendment. He begins by recognizing "the sincerity and integrity of the statements by the distinguished Senator from Wisconsin," and praises Nelson's leadership in the area of environment. Culver does respect Nelson for having been a leader in the field since long before it was a fashionable one. Then he answers a charge by Nelson that the compromise is a result of "panic." He argues that his own amendment strengthens the act—he can do this now that, as he planned, Stennis has been defeated—by requiring good-faith efforts to resolve conflicts and by requiring that a project be halted as soon as there is a realization that it might harm an endangered species. (Under the existing law, a project can be continued, as the Tellico Dam was, and thus a greater burden is placed on stopping it.) Culver rebuts Nelson on the facts, saying that it is probable that there will be an increasing number of conflicts under the act. As is his habit when he speaks, he paces back and forth within a small circle near his desk. He talks again about what he considers to be a major shortcoming in the way Congress addresses national questions: "If there is a problem with regard to the legislative process, given the nature of our current public-policy problems, it is our inability to anticipate problems and to get out and position ourselves responsibly and rationally in a way that, when the political pressures come, we will not do a shortsighted thing." He is clearly preoccupied with this problem; it is a rare legislator who even thinks about it.

Now his emotions—and his voice—are rising again, and it is late in the day, and he lets go with some other things that are on his mind. He asks, "What is a cheaper vote than to stand here in the Senate chamber and say, 'Nothing needs to be done'?" He begins to shout, his voice growing hoarse again: "There is no political constituency for common sense; there is no political constituency for standing in the middle of the cross fire and getting it from the right and getting it from the left." He warns that if a resolution of the issue is not agreed upon now, the act will be weakened in the future by bureaucratic, economic, and political pressures.

Then his frustration with some of the environmental groups—including some whose representatives are sitting in the gallery—spills out, and he says some things that politicians seldom say. "I would speak as someone who is really interested in the preservation and integrity of this act. We have had a number of environmental groups privately come in and whisper and wink and nod that this is what they want—'We think this will be very helpful'—but they know if they are going to get their dues every year they have to keep demagoguing to their constituency." He continues, "Well, I do not care how the votes fall on this one, but I say one thing: I hope they get the message. I am sick and tired of that kind of politics. I am sick and tired of it. I would like them, if they are worthy of representing these outstanding groups, to have the integrity to tell them the same thing they tell me. Unless and until they do, I am not interested in what they tell me." And, as if he realizes how far he has gone, he adds, "Very much." He praises the Audubon Society. (The Audubon Society has sent him a letter endorsing his approach and also saying, "We are aware of some of the heavy pressures that have been brought upon you from both sides and we want to commend you for your statesmanship and courage in trying to achieve a resolution that protects all aspects of the national interest.") Culver says, "That is one group that has put their money where their mouth is. They put their mouths where their constituency's money is. They have been honest and responsive and they follow the political climate. I think they know what is in their best interests." He returns to the subject of groups that are insatiable in their demands on even those politicians who are trying to help them—by doing the hard work of mediating. He says, "How long do they think we should walk the plank? How long can we have people who can possibly survive trying to do the right thing if they know we are doing the right thing and they speak out against us?" And he concludes by citing the quotation from John Dewey—"A man who prides himself upon acting upon principle is likely to be a man who insists upon having his own way without learning from experience what is the better way."

Nelson, knowing that his amendment would be defeated, withdraws it. He goes to Culver's desk, and the two men shake hands and joke with each other.

Now Culver's two greatest obstacles are out of the way, but he still has a number of amendments to deal with, and he cannot be sure that he knows about all that will be offered, so he cannot relax until the bill is put to a final vote.

At six-ten, William Scott calls up the first of a number of amendments he plans to offer. This one, Scott explains, is to provide that "the welfare of the human species be considered." It is this sort of amendment—which appears harmless but could do damage to the legislative history—against which managers of legislation have to be on guard. Fortunately for Culver, it is being offered by Scott, whose standing in the Senate is such that he attracts few votes for his proposals.

Culver responds to Scott, "The Congress and the U.S. Supreme Court have stated that the protection of endangered species is consistent with the welfare of the American people," and he adds, "The goals of the American people . . . are variable with time, and they often are not the same from person to person or . . . from senator to senator. What constitutes a proper goal for the welfare of the American people is a matter of constant debate." Scott's amendment is defeated on a roll-call vote of ten to eighty-six. He offers another one, specifying that an endangered species would be protected only if it was determined that it was of "substantial benefit to mankind."

In the course of Scott's remarks on behalf of this amendment, a young man in the gallery begins shouting. He has a superabundance of hair that flies in all directions, he is wearing a black T-shirt, and he has a rather wild look about him. "But that doesn't make any sense!" he shouts at Scott. "You can't tell what kinds of species are important to man!" The rest of the chamber is hushed. Interruptions from the gallery are not tolerated, and as the young man starts to go on some guards rush over and hustle him out.

Culver, rising to rebut Scott, looks down at the notes his staff has prepared for him on this amendment and sees that they suggest as his first argument, in effect, that Scott's proposal doesn't make any sense, that you can't tell what kinds of species are important to man. He hesitates, and begins somewhere else.

During the roll-call vote that follows, on Scott's

amendment, Culver gleefully goes about the floor telling his colleagues the story on himself. "I figured that either I should get that guy down here to debate Scott, or the guards were going to come down here and haul me out," he says. Each time he repeats the story, he laughs harder, sometimes doubling over. Scott's amendment is defeated, two to eighty-seven.

At seven-thirty, the Senate recesses for the evening, and will resume the debate at ten tomorrow morning. There was some thought of trying to complete action on the bill tonight, but too many amendments are still pending. Moreover, Scott has raised a couple of issues that have Culver worried. One is that Culver's proposal requires the presence of all seven members of the interagency committee for a quorum. On this, he thinks Scott has a point—the absence of one member could keep the committee from functioning. Also, Scott wants to amend the section of the bill which requires the votes of five of the seven members of the committee to exempt a project from the act; his amendment would require that only a majority is necessary. "Scott has opened something up," Culver says after he comes off the Senate floor. "There could be lots of amendments on the question of the quorum and how many votes are necessary. We deliberately loaded it so as to give the heavy presumption to the species. It's important to hold that. I've asked the staff to check for precedents for requiring a five-out-of-seven vote; they're not sure they can find any. I wish we could have kept the momentum going. There's a lot of momentum to these things. That's why it was important to defeat Stennis early. But it's harder to achieve momentum on this bill, because it's such a cross-quilt—so many amendments, coming from every direction. That's why we're trying to work out as many as we can informally."

Charles Stevenson meets Culver in the reception room off the Senate floor to go over the press release and give Culver materials for his press conference tomorrow on Soviet civil defense; when it was scheduled, Culver thought that the debate on the endangered-species bill would be over, or at least that the Senate would not be meeting in the morning. But it is getting toward the end of this year's session—it is an election year—and the legislation is piling up, so morning meetings are becoming frequent. Culver reads a note saying that William Hathaway wants his proxy for a vote in the Small Business Committee tomorrow. He asks Dick Oshlo to talk it over with Fred Holborn and Park Rinard, Culver's other senior staff member. Two people, representing the National Wildlife Federation and the Citizens Committee for Natural Resources, congratulate Culver on the job he did today, and Culver tells them that he appreciates their "constructive efforts." Neither of these is one of the groups that Culver was referring to on the floor this afternoon.

He thanks a representative of the Audubon Society for the letter. She tells Culver, "We took a lot of flak on it."

Culver replies, "I really appreciate that."

A staff member hands him a clipping from today's Des Moines *Register* which says that a rare clam—the *Lampsilis higginsi*, or Higgins' eye—has been found in the Mississippi River, near the site of a proposed bridge outside Dubuque.

This evening, Culver goes to Nelson's home for dinner. (He does not have time to stop by, as he hoped to, at a fund-raising reception for an old friend of his in the House.) Nelson and his wife, Carrie Lee—a woman much admired for her frankness—are hospitable people, and tonight they have gathered a number of senators and other friends. Nelson and Culver kid each other a good bit during the evening. Nelson teases Culver about how long his speech was early this afternoon; Culver tells the story on himself about the young man in the gallery. Nelson lobbies Culver on some amendments he will offer tomorrow, telling him they will strengthen his hand when he goes to conference, and then he kids Culver again about his speech. "You son of a bitch," Nelson says. "You used my arguments." Nelson and Culver laugh.

11

WEDNESDAY, JULY 19TH: Culver has gone to the White House for the eight-o'clock breakfast meeting on lifting the embargo on the sale of arms to Turkey (he asked the President to what extent the policy of lifting the embargo, in the interests of strengthening NATO, had anticipated a negative reaction in Greece, which could have consequences that would weaken NATO); at nine-thirty, he met on the Senate steps with 4-H Clubs from three counties in Iowa; at nine-forty-five, he met with Charles Stevenson to go over some questions he had on the material, which he had read early this morning, for the press conference on Soviet civil defense; and then he met with George Jacobson and Kathi Korpon on amendments that will come up today on the endangered-species bill.

Now, at ten o'clock, the Senate resumes debate on the bill. S. I. Hayakawa, Republican of California, offers a minor amendment, which Culver accepts, in accordance with his policy of accepting as many as he can in order to build a consensus behind the bill. Representatives of the Fish and Wildlife Service are stationed in the Vice President's Capitol Hill office, off the Senate floor, and amendments that Culver is giving consideration to accepting are sent out to them for their opinion. He turns the floor over to Wallop so that Wallop can engage Hayakawa in a colloquy to establish the legislative history of the amendment. Culver is giving Wallop a larger role than the majority manager usually affords the minority—also in the interest of building a consensus.

Shortly before ten-thirty, Culver leaves the floor to go to the Dirksen Office Building for his press conference on Soviet civil defense. Just before the press conference begins, he goes over again with Charles Stevenson the points he wants to stress. A fair number of newspaper reporters are here, along with reporters from two television networks and one television station in Iowa. Culver enters the room and sits behind a table that has several microphones on it. He is wearing a navy-blue suit, a blue shirt, and a navy-blue tie with small white dots. He reads a statement explaining that "for the past two years I have sought an official but unclassified assessment of Soviet civil defense which could be made available for a better-informed public debate on this issue." The report he has received, and is releasing today, he says, "represents the first comprehensive and authoritative analysis of this crucial topic in unclassified form." He says that "the study indicates that the Soviet civil-defense system, while representing a significant national effort, is by no means sufficiently effective to encourage the Soviets to risk starting a nuclear war."

He continues, "While crediting the Soviet Union with a major, ongoing civil-defense program, this report demonstrates that those efforts are not sufficient to prevent millions of casualties and massive industrial damage in the event of a nuclear war. In short, Soviet programs are not enough to tip the strategic balance against us." He is addressing himself to recent alarms that the Soviets are engaged in a new civil-defense effort of sufficient proportions that the strategic balance might indeed be tipped, and to arguments that therefore the United States should also engage in a new, enlarged civil-defense program. Now, also addressing himself to the arguments of critics of SALT, and pursuing his goal, about which he spoke to me earlier, of achieving more understanding in both the United States and the Soviet Union concerning the consequences of a nuclear exchange, he says, "Despite the widespread claims that Soviet leaders might launch a nuclear attack because they expect to suffer only moderate damage and few casualties—and we hear that suggested today in a number of quarters—the professional judgment of our intelligence community is that they would not be emboldened to expose themselves and their country to a higher risk of nuclear attack. Even under the 'worst case' assumptions of this study, nuclear war would be a disaster for the Soviet Union." He takes questions, and answers earnestly and with a large number of facts. He says that the estimates of each side's losses in a nuclear attack vary with the targeting plan and the warning time—that the Soviet Union could lose well over a hundred million people, but that that figure could be cut by more than fifty per cent if it had two to three days' warning. "I guess the bottom line in all this," he says, "is that even in the worst case the casualties would be awesome."

When one of the reporters questions his conclusions, Culver becomes annoyed. "We do have a great deal of speculation. It's rampant," he says, referring to the alarms about the nature of the Soviet threat. His voice rises. "We don't need to panic," he says. "There is no surge planning. Since they can't have high confidence—and that's what this report is about—the Soviet Union would not be emboldened to risk a nuclear war." Culver is getting involved, and he just keeps going, making his argument, ranging into the way he thinks about the whole subject. He may have a bill pending on the Senate floor, but now he gives this his all, takes the opportunity to present his case. He says, "We talk so much about military doctrine—that General So-and-So says this, that General So-and-So says that. Soldiers in every country all the time talk about victory. They're not paid to talk about defeat. They are trained with the can-do spirit, and the can-do spirit can lead to nuclear war—holocaust, believe it or not." The passion has come to the surface again. "The political leadership on both sides believe that nuclear war would be a disaster," he says. "Now, whether the troops have got the message is another question." Addressing himself to his questioner, he continues, "The Soviet civil-defense effort, I beg your pardon, is not the coördinated, effective system that some so-called experts have claimed, according to the judgment of the people who wrote this report." He goes on—as he did with me in his office, as he did with the constituents in Des Moines—about both sides having civil-defense signs in their subways, both sides having pamphlets. He says, "If you just like to embrace rumor and innuendo and fear, fine. Some people make a lifetime career of it."

He then tries to turn to someone else, but the reporter follows up with a question based on a statement by a Soviet general.

"I could probably provide you with some statements by our highest military or some article they've written," Culver replies. "In that context, everyone's talking about, quote, winning a war, unquote."

He goes on for a while, talking about Soviet history. "I'm not minimizing their effort, and it may be comfortable to characterize my position as 'weak on civil defense,' " he says, "but what I want to do is to get objective information before the public."

In answer to a question about whether he thinks that the United States should proceed to spend substantially increased funds on civil defense over the next few years, Culver says, "I think that we're just going to have to carefully look at it and review it." He adds that he thinks this is an area that should be explored in future SALT talks. "It seems to me that before we all pour a lot of money along this line," he says, "why don't we get together and try to agree, in the spirit of the A.B.M. agreement"—in 1972, the United States and the Soviet Union agreed to limit substantially their deployment of anti-ballistic missiles—"and try to find a way to minimize the threat." This is how he argued in opposing construction of a military base on Diego Garcia, and later there were talks on demilitarizing the Indian Ocean; this is how he argued about conventional-arms sales, and later there were talks on that subject. However fruitful the talks may or may not be, Culver considers such efforts worth a try.

Culver concludes the press conference at eleven-fifteen.

In an anteroom, Don Brownlee is waiting with a tape-recording machine, so that Culver can record "actualities" to send out to the Iowa radio stations. As Brownlee holds a microphone, Culver reads two excerpts from his statement. Charles Stevenson tells Culver that he has some questions about provisions that Culver backed which might come up in the House-Senate conference on the military-procurement bill this afternoon—questions about which provisions he might want to trade for what. "We'll have to talk about that more, Charlie," Culver says.

When Culver returns to the Senate floor, an amendment by Nelson is pending. This one would limit projects that could be exempted to those for which "a substantial and irretrievable commitment of resources had been made." Culver speaks in opposition, saying that the amendment "does have some superficial appeal" but could have undesirable results—that it could have the effect of discouraging agencies from confronting the problem until a project was well along. He does an imitation, in a prissy voice, of an imagined, unrealistic statement by a representative of the Fish and Wildlife Service in the course of a discussion over whether a project should proceed. He draws an analogy—perhaps because of what he was dealing with in his press conference—between such discussions and the bargaining over SALT. "This amendment could have the force and effect of accelerating the move toward construction," he says. "This amendment says the only way you can have any hope for receiving an exemption is to get in there and build." He cites Nelson's proposed language—"a substantial and irretrievable commitment of resources." He bellows, "What on earth is that? Is there a lawyer in the house? Substantial to whom? Irretrievable to whom?" He returns to the defense analogy, referring now to the current controversy over whether and what sort of a mobile-missile system should be built. "We may have to dig a hole where the Furbish lousewort lives," he says, and he goes on to say that we should not get into a situation where it would be like saying to the Defense Department, " 'Go ahead and build the damn thing, and if you build it enough to spend thirty million dollars, then we will tell you you should not have done it in the first place.' " Nelson's amendment is defeated by a vote of twenty-five to seventy.

During the roll call, Culver goes over to the Republican side to confer with Scott.

Now Scott offers an amendment to exempt a project that might prevent the recurrence of a natural disaster, and Culver accepts it. Scott previously referred several times in the debate to a flood in Virginia that took the lives of four people, and yesterday afternoon Culver decided to try to reach agreement with him on an amendment to cover natural disasters. Next, he accepts an amendment by Scott to provide that five rather than all seven members of the interagency committee will constitute a quorum. Culver's hope is that if he accommodates Scott, Scott may reciprocate by withholding some of the several amendments he still has pending. "It's like a negotiating situation," Culver has explained to me. "You have twelve amendments, but there are only three or four you care about." Scott, however, is unpredictable. And though Scott has little influence within the Senate, Culver still has to be concerned that, as the day goes on, the Senate might accept something that Scott proposes or an atmosphere might be created in which some surprise amendment would be adopted. When Senate sessions go on until late in the day or into the evening, matters can get increasingly out of hand: tempers rise, a few drinks may have been consumed, and a certain "what the hell?" attitude can take over. "Late in the day gets to be the silly season," Culver has explained to me. "It gets harder and harder to control what happens."

For that reason, Culver has persuaded Scott to bring up now the amendment that Culver most fears: the one to require a majority vote, rather than a vote of five of the seven members, of the interagency committee in granting an exemption. He is worried that his proposal is vulnerable here. And he is concerned that if the number of votes required to exempt a project should be reduced to a simple majority many more projects might be exempted. Scott was not enthusiastic about offering the amendment at this point, but Culver has talked him into it. The theory behind having Scott bring up the amendment now is that it is better to have such a proposal come up in the morning—a time when many senators are in committee meetings or in their offices and are more distracted than usual from the business that is taking place on the floor. Also, Culver figures that most of his colleagues will assume that at this point, especially after a long day of taking up amendments—and major ones—yesterday, only routine, "housekeeping" amendments are being considered, and that they will pay less attention to the issue, be less eager to join the fray, than they might be later on.

These are the sorts of calculations that managers of bills must make. Culver figures, further, that if an amendment is to be offered on the voting of the new committee he would prefer that it be offered by Scott. And, by a prior arrangement that Culver has made with Nelson, Nelson will ask for a roll-call vote on the amendment. Scott does not want a roll call on it. Culver's idea is to beat the amendment, and beat it good, burying the issue in the Senate once and for all, and also putting him in a position to tell a Senate-House conference on the bill that the proposal was resoundingly defeated in the Senate. "It's a judgment call," Culver has said, explaining to me the considerations behind whether or not to put something to a roll-call vote. Sometimes, as happened when Stennis, as chairman of the Armed Services Committee and floor manager of the military-procurement bill, accepted Culver's amendment on aircraft carriers, a senator will decide not to press for a roll-call vote, to—as Culver puts it—"God, take it and run."

So now Scott calls up his amendment to require that the votes of only four of the seven members of the interagency committee are necessary in order to exempt a project. Culver, speaking in opposition to the amendment, offers some precedents for requiring a "super-majority" vote. Culver wasn't sure there were any precedents, but his staff has been imaginative: he uses the example of jury trials in criminal cases—which require unanimity—and he cites the Senate rule that a filibuster can be cut off only by the votes of sixty members, or three-fifths, of the Senate. Scott's amendment is defeated on a roll-call vote, twenty-three to sixty-nine.

Now Culver accepts a number of other amendments offered by Republicans. He has told me, "You can take a couple of amendments you know you are going to drop in a spittoon on the way to the conference." Nelson had some other amendments, too, but by one-thirty he and the environmentalists backing him have decided to give up.

Off the Senate floor, a Democratic senator talks to me about Culver. "He's doing a real good job of managing the bill," the senator says. "It's a controversial issue; he's picking his way through the amendments, and working some out, and fighting and defeating others, and establishing his control over the floor. That's very important: others will follow your lead if they feel that you're being sensible and you have control."

This afternoon, Culver—he has skipped lunch again—works to keep that control. He quickly moves against a senator who has asked for more time than was permitted under the unanimous-consent agreement and who wants to offer a non-germane amendment.

While another senator is speaking, Culver leaves the floor briefly; he has received a card of the sort that visitors send in when they want to see senators, this one telling him that a delegation of forty-one Catholics from Dubuque would like to see him. (He has turned down a number of other requests today to meet with people off the Senate floor.) He goes over to the Rotunda of the Capitol and meets with the group for five minutes, explaining to them that he is managing a bill on the Senate floor, and adding, "I figured if I didn't come out to see you, you'd fire me, but if I don't get back in there the Majority Leader will fire me."

When Culver returns to the Senate, Wallop is sitting next to Scott's seat, in the second-to-last row, talking to Scott, and Culver goes back to join them. After he accepted Scott's amendments this morning, Culver told him that he hoped that that would take care of matters and that Scott would offer no further amendments. Scott said then that he wanted to go back to his office and look over his other amendments. This afternoon, he returned to say that he had four more he wanted to offer, and Culver asked Wallop to go back and talk to Scott and see what he could do. Now Culver finds that they haven't got very far; Scott is insisting that either he be allowed to offer four amendments or he will ultimately offer twelve. Culver has asked for a quorum call—a device used from time to time during a debate in order to gain time to get a senator to the floor, or to regroup, or to work out an amendment, or to negotiate—and the clerk calls the roll, slowly. At one point during the negotiations, Culver puts his head in his hands, seeming very weary.

Finally, at five minutes to three, Culver comes back to his desk and asks that the quorum call be ended. He has talked Scott into offering just one more amendment. Now Scott offers one providing that if the National Security Council determines that any interference with a critical military installation on behalf of an endangered species "would have an adverse effect on the security of the United States," it is authorized to notify the interagency committee in writing and that "the committee shall give immediate consideration to such determination." In the preceding negotiations, Culver has succeeded in getting Scott to modify this amendment; in its original form, it would have allowed the National Security Council to grant an automatic exemption, and it would have been invoked to prevent an adverse effect on any installation, not just one deemed essential to the national security. Culver's objections were that anything might be found adverse to an installation and that granting an automatic exemption was contrary to the spirit of the bill.

Now Scott says, "Suppose a bird or some endangered species was in front of an intercontinental ballistic missile. They could not release that missile." He goes on to say that he thinks "any commander worth his salt" would go ahead and fire the missile, but that, under the Endangered Species Act, the commander would then "be subject to a fine of twenty thousand dollars and imprisonment for up to a year."

Culver, who appears to be struggling to keep a straight face, commends Scott, saying that his amendment "is extremely important and is acceptable."

Then, just as the debate is nearing its end, the Senate sets aside the endangered-species bill to take up the Quiet Communities Act of 1978—the noise-control bill that Culver had talked about in Des Moines, and that he must also manage. Culver is waiting for a certain senator to reach the floor to offer an amendment to the endangered-species bill, and he knows that the noise-control bill is noncontroversial and will take little time, so he and Byrd have decided to bring it up now. Arrangements of this sort are made from time to time, both to accommodate senators and to move legislation along. After Culver reads a statement explaining the provisions of the noise-control bill, it is adopted by voice vote, and the Senate returns to the endangered-species bill, and the last pending amendment is offered and withdrawn.

Now Wallop and Culver commend each other, and their own staffs, on the work on the bill, a few other senators make brief statements, and the roll is called on final passage.

It is clear that the bill will pass, so during the roll call Culver leaves the floor. Don Brownlee has asked him to meet on a grassy spot in front of the Capitol with Dean Norland, a television correspondent from Cedar Rapids. Norland has to have his film at the airport by four o'clock in order to get it on tonight's news.

It is one of those hot, humid Washington summer afternoons. "Hi, Dean," Culver says to Norland. "Can we do this before your subject melts?"

Norland asks him what this bill will do for Iowa, and makes specific reference to the problem of the Dubuque bridge and the Higgins' eye clam.

Culver explains that the bill would require a consultation process. He stands with his hands folded in front of him, and has his somber look; he talks firmly and with composure. There is no sign of how hot and tired he is. The bill, he says, "represents a responsible and rational balance of competing needs, with a strong presumption in favor, whenever there is doubt, of the endangered species." He talks a bit longer, says, "Thank you, Dean, 'preciate it," and then says, "I think I'll go see how my vote is."

On the way back, he glances at his schedule card and notices that he was to meet a constituent for a handshake at three o'clock. He asks Brownlee, "What happened to that constituent?" Brownlee isn't sure. Culver reads a memorandum Brownlee has given him about phone calls that have come in for him: James Schlesinger, the Secretary of Energy, has called him, and so has Patricia Harris, the Secretary of Housing and Urban Development.

When Culver reaches the Senate floor, the roll call is just about completed, and in a few moments Adlai Stevenson, who is presiding, gives the final tally. "On this vote," he says, "the yeas are ninety-four and the nays are three." Culver allows himself a smile of satisfaction, but quickly suppresses it and accepts the congratulations of his colleagues.

It is now shortly after four, and, after going into the cloakroom to talk with some of his colleagues and unwind for a few minutes, Culver goes to the President's Room, a small room behind the Senate floor, to meet Bill Griffee, an Iowa state representative from Nashua, who has been attempting to obtain funds from the Department of Energy to revitalize an old power-dam system. "What would you like me to do at this stage, Bill?" Culver asks.

Griffee replies, "I would like you to keep track of the people in the Department of Energy." Jim Larew, who has accompanied Griffee here, takes notes. Griffee continues, "It just helps if they know a United States senator is darned interested."

Culver offers to make calls when Griffee thinks it would be helpful, and Griffee asks whether he has any objections if when he talks to the press he says that he has spoken with Senator Culver about this project. Culver says, "No, that's all right," and he adds, "I'm not familiar with all the feelings about the project." Don Brownlee takes a picture of the two men standing together.

It is now four-twenty. Jim Larew gives Culver a memorandum from Mike Naylor, Culver's legislative director, telling him that tomorrow the Administration will announce its position on product-liability insurance for small businesses, and that it will fall short of what Culver has proposed. He suggests that Culver get ready to respond to the Administration's announcement, and asks whether, if Culver does not have time to receive a briefing on it this afternoon—he doesn't—Naylor may tell Commerce Department staff members that Culver has asked that Naylor be briefed on the details. Culver writes "Yes" on the memorandum. An aide sends word that today the Agriculture Appropriations Subcommittee has approved one hundred million dollars for Culver's soil-conservation, clean-water program. Brownlee gives him a note saying that a certain part of the military-procurement bill is coming up in conference at four-thirty. Culver decides that if it is important enough one of his colleagues will send word asking him to come.

Now Culver proceeds to the Radio and Television Gallery to talk about the endangered-species bill. This is routine for major figures in a legislative battle. Culver goes into a room containing a set that consists of a mock office. He sits at a desk, with rows of maroon-bound volumes of the *Congressional Record* behind him. There are blue drapes on either side, and Culver pops a cigar that he has been smoking—the cigar is one small way to relieve the tension—on a shelf behind one of the drapes. ABC and CBS are here, and so are several radio reporters.

The first question is "Senator Culver, why did you find it necessary to weaken this act?"

Culver replies carefully—and evenly, under the circumstances—"I don't think we've weakened this act. I think we effected a compromise that would enable it to continue at all. Our subcommittee's hearings indicated that either it would be compromised or it wouldn't be reauthorized at all or it would be emasculated." He explains the bill. This is his best opportunity to explain publicly what it is about. He hasn't had lunch, and he's very tired—he hasn't stopped going all day—but now he states clearly and with energy why the bill was necessary. He draws on his capacity for discipline one more time. He tells how the inflexibility of the existing law had inhibited the Fish and Wildlife Service in carrying it out, and says, "So if you're really concerned about endangered species you've got to be concerned about inflexibility in the law." He stresses the point that through the requirement for five out of seven votes in the committee "the presumption is heavily in favor of the species."

A reporter says that he has had trouble with his tape recorder, and asks Culver if he will explain it all again.

Culver's eyes roll upward, but he coöperates. Then he says, "I hope what we've done is get out ahead of this problem a little bit."

He takes a few more questions, and ends the press conference and retrieves his cigar.

Over coffee in the Senate dining room, Culver talks about the day and goes over some of the messages he has been given. A State Department official is trying to reach him in connection with the proposal to lift the embargo on the sale of arms to Turkey; Howard Metzenbaum is trying to reach him in connection with a torts bill that is pending before the Judiciary Committee. Culver looks at a memorandum about the torts bill. "Doesn't it all just defy belief?" he says to me.

It is now six o'clock. The Senate has taken up the authorization bill for the Department of Housing and Urban Development and is still in session. Later, Culver will go to a fund-raiser for a friend of his who is running for attorney general of Iowa. Tomorrow, he is scheduled to go at eight o'clock to a breakfast seminar on SALT; and then attend a hearing of the Environmental Pollution Subcommittee; and meet with Dr. Norman Borlaug, who is from Iowa, and who received a Nobel Peace Prize for his development of high-yield grain (the "green revolution"); and then meet with Josy Gittler about bills pending before his Juvenile Delinquency Subcommittee; and then have lunch with his two daughters who are in Washington (this weekend, he will go back to McGregor); and then attend the House-Senate conference on the military-procurement bill and also a meeting of the Environment and Public

Works Committee on a bill that is part of the President's economic stimulus program (these two meetings will overlap); and meet with a constituent for a handshake; and, of course, go to the Senate floor to vote.

INDEX

About the Author

Elizabeth Drew is a journalist in Washington and a regular contributor to *The New Yorker*. Her articles have also appeared in *The New York Times* and *The Atlantic*, for which she was the Washington editor for six years, and have been published in some thirty anthologies.

In addition to her work as a writer, Ms. Drew is a commentator for the *Washington Post-Newsweek* stations, appears regularly on "Agronsky and Company," and often participates in other nationally televised public-affairs shows. From 1971 to 1973 she hosted her own television interview program on the Public Broadcasting Service. In 1976 she was selected for the first panel of questioners in the Presidential debates. She has won many awards for her work, including the Award for Excellence from the Society of Magazine Writers, the Dupont-Columbia Award for Broadcast Journalism, the *Ladies' Home Journal* award as Woman of the Year in Communications (1977) and, in 1979, the Medal for Distinguished Service to Journalism from the University of Missouri's School of Journalism.

Born in Cincinnati, she is a graduate of Wellesley College and has been awarded honorary degrees from Yale University, Hood College, and Trinity College in Washington.